COME MEET JESUS

An Invitation from
POPE BENEDICT XVI

AMY WELBORN

COME MEET JESUS

An Invitation from
POPE BENEDICT XVI

AMY WELBORN

theWORD
among us®
Press

Published by The Word Among Us Press
9639 Doctor Perry Road
Ijamsville, Maryland 21754
www.wordamongus.org

14 13 12 11 10   1 2 3 4 5

ISBN: 978-1-59325-167-3

Cover design by John Hamilton Designs

Library of Congress Cataloging-in-Publication Data
Welborn, Amy.
  Come meet Jesus : an invitation from Pope Benedict XVI / Amy Welborn.
    p. cm.
  Includes bibliographical references (p.   ).
  ISBN 978-1-59325-167-3
  1. Jesus Christ--Person and offices. 2. Benedict XVI, Pope, 1927- I. Title.
  BT203.W425 2010
  232'.8--dc22
                              2009039207

TABLE OF CONTENTS

INTRODUCTION

Pope Benedict XVI has preached many homilies, delivered dozens of speeches, and conveyed regular messages to the Church and the world.

He has spoken to hundreds of thousands of young people around the world, to small groups of the sick and disabled, to ambassadors, university faculties, priests and religious, children, the faithful gathered at places of pilgrimages, and the curious stopping by St. Peter's Square on a warm Wednesday morning, wondering who this fellow is and what all the fuss could be about.

Is it possible to pull a common thread from this rich, diverse body of works?

I believe it is, and this book is the fruit of that conviction.

His fellow academics have correctly discerned many fundamental themes in the work of theologian Joseph Ratzinger: an interest in the relationship between faith and reason, religion and culture, modernity and faith; the liturgy; and the continuity and discontinuity in historical development.

A pope does not leave his own interests and expertise at the door of the Sistine Chapel when he is elected, so all these points of study that interested Joseph Ratzinger over his decades as an academic theologian continue to inform his writing as pope.

However, when you listen and read the papal writings attentively, it is difficult not to notice one particular element that seems to come into focus no matter what the specific topic or who the audience is.

That "element" is a person: Jesus Christ.

Benedict made this focus clear from his first homily as pope. He referred to Pope John Paul II's 1978 inaugural homily in which his predecessor exhorted his listeners to "Open wide the doors for Christ." Benedict concluded his own homily in this way:

> If we let Christ into our lives, we lose nothing, nothing, absolutely nothing of what makes life free, beautiful, and great. No! Only in this friendship are the doors of life opened wide. Only in this friendship is the great potential of human existence truly revealed. Only in this friendship do we experience beauty and liberation. And so, today, with great strength and great conviction, on the basis of long personal experience of life, I say to you, dear young people: Do not be afraid of Christ! He takes nothing away, and he gives you everything. When we give ourselves to him, we receive a hundredfold in return. Yes, open, open wide the doors to Christ—and you will find true life.[1]

Pope Benedict has articulated this invitation countless times over the years of his pontificate. Whether the initial occasion concerns liturgy, vocations, justice and charity, or a particular moment in the Church's year, for the Holy Father, everything always comes back to Jesus Christ. It is in Jesus, the pope reminds us, that we find the peace for which our anxious, restless hearts yearn. In him we find joy and comfort when the world lets us down. It is in him that we find the true, lasting answers to the anxieties and fears that beset us all in the darkest nights and in the midst of the most intense suffering.

Come Meet Jesus highlights the ways in which Pope Benedict is inviting his listeners, both inside and outside the Catholic Church, to discover the saving, healing, life-giving love of Jesus. Pope Benedict's words are not difficult to understand. He writes in a lucid, clear style. However, as I mentioned at the beginning, the quantity of works available from even a few years of his papacy is great, and not many of us have the time to follow the pope's words on a daily basis. This book is offered with the hope that more might be inspired to listen with open minds and hearts to Pope Benedict's persistent and heartfelt invitation for all of us to put friendship with Jesus at the center of our lives.

Amy Welborn

CHAPTER ONE

MEETING POPE BENEDICT

*And now, at this moment, weak servant of God that I am,
I must assume this enormous task, which truly exceeds all
human capacity. How can I do this? How will I be able to do
it? All of you, my dear friends, have just invoked the entire
host of saints, represented by some of the great names in the
history of God's dealings with mankind. In this way, I too can
say with renewed conviction: I am not alone. I do not have
to carry alone what in truth I could never carry alone. All the
saints of God are there to protect me, to sustain me, and to
carry me. And your prayers, my dear friends, your indulgence,
your love, your faith, and your hope accompany me.*[2]

Before we explore Pope Benedict's words in more depth, it will be helpful to get a better sense of the man himself.

This is especially important because, despite his fame, not many people have a complete understanding of who Pope Benedict XVI is beyond some very basic facts. And unfortunately, we sometimes hear things that are twisted by an unsympathetic or even hostile observer, giving us an unfair and inaccurate caricature of him.

Knowing a bit about Pope Benedict's life and intellectual interests will help us as we listen to what he has to tell us about Jesus. We'll be able to see how the way he speaks about friendship with Jesus flows naturally from his own life experiences as well as from his chosen areas of study and research.

Pope Benedict speaks regularly and with great conviction about what friendship with Jesus really means. He does not do so because it's his job or because he wants to educate us about some interesting concepts. Pope Benedict invites us to friendship with Jesus because he is moved by the truth that forms his own life, a life marked by that very friendship at its center, nourished in the context of the richness of Catholic spiritual tradition as well as his own intellectual journey.

Early Life: God in the Details

Joseph Ratzinger was born in Martkl am Inn in northern Bavaria, the heavily Catholic area of southern Germany. He was the youngest child of Joseph and Maria Ratzinger, having one older sister, Maria, and an older brother, Georg.

The date of his birth is April 16, 1927, which was Holy Saturday that year, and Joseph was baptized just a few hours after his birth on the same day, with the waters blessed at the Easter Vigil service. Any of us would probably find meaning in such a confluence of events, and in his memoir, *Milestones*, Joseph Ratzinger described the impact it had on him:

> To be the first person baptized with the new water was seen as a significant act of Providence. I have always been filled with thanksgiving for having had my life immersed in this way in the Easter Mystery . . . the more I reflect on it, the more this seems fitting for the nature of our human life: we are still waiting for Easter; we are not yet standing in the full light but walking toward it full of trust.[3]

Joseph Ratzinger Sr. was a police officer, and the family moved around quite a bit in those early years. By the pope's own account, his childhood, while not enriched by material wealth, was a happy one. His memories are marked by a sense of gratitude: gratitude for his loving parents, for the opportunities to learn, for the natural flow of seasons, as well as for the richness of Catholic faith and devotion that surrounded him in the culture in which he was growing up.

In his memoir, he touches on these recollections: of pilgrimages to popular shrines, to restful afternoons in natural enclaves, of the place of churches, monasteries, and convents in community life. Ratzinger's appreciation of all of these riches is not grounded in nostalgia for a past world in which the Church functioned as a fortress or a ghetto. No, it is simply that through these experiences and realities, he encountered the presence of God. In these small moments of "incarnation," the greater and more fundamental incarnation of the Word made flesh is echoed. God can be touched in his creation as well as in the objects of beauty that human beings create themselves. They all reveal God's own beauty to us and enable us to catch a glimpse of the eternal. Art, music, liturgical devotions, and even simple memories of ordinary life evoked God's presence in the life of Joseph Ratzinger.

I have a very clear memory of one of my visits to Altötting. It was a cold day, and I was crossing the large square, heading toward the famous chapel. The restricted space inside was overcrowded. Candles were burning everywhere in the semi-darkness. The chapel was filled almost exclusively with women praying and singing Marian hymns. I sensed that this was a way not just to overcome my weaknesses, but also to find renewed strength.[4]

Our parents helped us from early on to understand the liturgy. There was a children's prayerbook adapted from the missal in which the unfolding of the sacred action was portrayed in pictures, so we could follow closely what was happening. Next to each picture there was a simple prayer that summarized the essentials of each part of the liturgy and adapted it to a child's mode of prayer. I was then given a *Schott* for children, in which the liturgy's basic texts themselves were printed. Then I got a *Schott* for Sundays, which contained the complete liturgy for Sundays and feast days. Finally, I received the complete missal for every day of the year.

Every new step into the liturgy was a great event for me. Each new book I was given was something precious to me, and I could not dream of anything more beautiful. It was a riveting adventure to move by degrees into the mysterious world of the liturgy, which was being enacted before us and for us there on the altar. It was becoming more and more clear to me that here I was encountering a reality that no one had simply thought up, a reality that no official authority or great individual had created. This mysterious fabric of texts and actions had grown from the faith of the Church over the centuries. It bore the whole weight of history within itself, and yet, at the same time, it was much more than the product of human history. Every century had left its mark upon it. The introductory notes informed us about what came from the early Church, what from the Middle Ages, and what from modern times. Not everything was logical. Things sometimes got complicated, and it was not always easy to find one's way. But precisely this is what made the whole edifice wonderful, like one's own home. Naturally, the child I then was did not grasp every aspect of this, but I started down the road of the liturgy, and this became a continuous process of growth into a grand reality transcending all particular individuals and generations, a reality that became an occasion for me of ever-new amazement and discovery.[5]

It is worth quoting these passages at length, for in them we encounter, not only Pope Benedict's strong interest in the prayer and liturgical life of the Church, but also his gift of being able to explain the spiritual realities evoked by the things of this earth: by buildings, by ritual, even by nature. As you will see in the following pages, when Pope Benedict gives a homily as a visitor in a church building, he often frames the homily in an exploration of the architecture and art of the structure. He draws meaning from the symbols and rituals attached to the occasion on which he is preaching. From childhood he was able to discern the ways in which God uses human realities to communicate his loving, merciful presence: God's trustworthiness, his beauty, and, as the description of the pilgrimage to Altötting shows so simply, as a place to be nourished and to find strength. As a preacher and teacher, helping his listeners make these connections as well has been an essential element of his approach. We'll encounter this deeply sacramental vision again.

Schooling

Joseph Ratzinger attended school during the rise of the Third Reich, and his account of his youthful education is marked by memories of stress, tension, conflict, and change as the regime slowly but surely made its mark on the formation of the young. Religious subjects and practice gradually disappeared, replaced by reverence for the Reich, the Führer, and vaguely pagan practices. Some teachers cooperated; others resisted, refusing to have their students sing anti-Semitic songs, and were replaced. Children were forced into compulsory membership in the Hitler Youth, including the Ratzinger brothers. It is essential to note, however, that contrary to what some suggest, the Ratzingers were not Nazis. Joseph Ratzinger Sr. was never a member of the Nazi party and was, in fact, a fierce opponent of all aspects of the regime from its inception in the early 1930s to the very end of the war, taking the great risk of criticizing the regime directly to two SS men who had forced the family to quarter them.

In 1939 Joseph Ratzinger began attending a minor seminary some distance from home, but later that year, the seminary was taken over to serve as a military hospital, and it had to move to other quarters. Life continued under increasing financial pressure, and in 1943, the war hit home as Georg was drafted into military service. Soon after, sixteen-year-old Joseph, along with the rest of his seminary classmates, was brought into the conflict.

Ratzinger was forced to serve in three capacities during the last fifteen months of World War II. He was initially brought in on anti-aircraft duties, and taken to Munich along with other schoolboys who were all allowed to continue school part time. He was then placed on labor duty, and then, in late 1944, put through basic training. He was never in direct conflict, and describes this last stage as essentially a series of endless training and drilling.

And then, he writes simply and strikingly in his memoir, "At the end of April or the beginning of May—I do not remember precisely—I decided to go home."[6] In short, he made the decision to desert. Although the war was essentially over by this point (Germany signed the documents of unconditional surrender on May 7, 1945), the act was still, if discovered, punishable by death.

Ratzinger made it home safely, but tensions and fears could not abate until the Americans reached the home village, which they soon did, and began rounding up German military as POWs. Ratzinger spent that early summer of 1945 as a prisoner of war of the Americans, was released in June, and then, with the rest of his family, welcomed his brother Georg home in July.

It is clear that those who would refer to Joseph Ratzinger as a Nazi are being not only inaccurate but deeply unfair, even untruthful. The Ratzinger family suffered under the Nazi regime. They suffered as Church institutions were suppressed and as the freedom to express one's faith was stripped away. They suffered from the effects of the war, and, it has recently been revealed, they suffered directly. One of their cousins, who was born with Down syndrome, was removed from his home by the Nazis, taken for "therapy," and died soon after, as happened to so many other people with disabilities.

As we read Pope Benedict, we will frequently encounter discussions of the relationship between faith and culture, between religion and society, and between religion and the powers of this world. Pope Benedict does not deny the complexity of these relationships, but neither does he ever fail to emphasize the necessity of staying faithful to Christ above all else. He often writes of the consequences for a society when it forgets God and seeks to construct life around ideologies that place humanity and its power to control at the center of existence rather than respect for God and his creation. The tragic irony, he notes again and again, is that systems that reject God end up being the systems most oppressive of human beings.

We walk in a world that is often plagued by darkness. In that world, only one constant light of goodness and hope shines: Jesus Christ. When we listen to Pope Benedict speak to us in the twenty-first century, we will find that his experiences in oppressive regimes of the twentieth century play a role as he reminds us to hold fast to Christ in the midst of any darkness that surrounds us.

An Academic Career

Both Joseph and Georg Ratzinger were ordained priests on June 29, 1951, in the cathedral at Freising, Germany. After his ordination, Fr. Ratzinger continued his studies, receiving his doctorate in theology from the University of Munich in 1953. A few years later, he published a study that qualified him to teach at the university level. The subject of his doctoral dissertation was St. Augustine of Hippo's theology of the Church, and a later study looked at St. Bonaventure's study of the theology of history.

From this point through 1977, Fr. Ratzinger's ministry was a combination of teaching and pastoral work. He held positions in Bonn, Münster, Tübingen, and Regensburg, teaching courses centered on subjects such as dogmatic theology, revelation, the nature of the Church, and sacrament and Scripture.

He was, by all accounts, a very popular teacher. Former students recalled:

> The lectures were prepared down to the millimeter. He gave them by paraphrasing the text that he'd prepared with formulations that at times seemed to fit together like a mosaic, with a wealth of images that reminded me of Romano Guardini. In some lectures, as in the pauses in a concert, you could have heard a pin drop. The Redemptorist Viktor Hahn, who was the first student to "doctor" himself with Ratzinger, adds: "The room was always packed, the students adored him. He had a beautiful and simple language. The language of a believer."[7]

Another former student recounted that Ratzinger's preparation often involved reading his lectures to his sister, Maria, who was living with him during these years. When she understood the content, the lectures were ready to deliver to students.

It was during this time that Ratzinger's first book was published. *Introduction to Christianity* was the fruit of a lecture series on the Apostles' Creed, tape-recorded by an assistant and transcribed. It went through ten printings in its first year of publication.

Aside from his teaching, one of Ratzinger's most significant activities during the 1960s was his participation in the Second Vatican Council. He attended all the sessions of the council as the theological advisor to Cardinal Joseph Frings of Cologne.

When we listen to Pope Benedict today, we are listening to

a style and emphasis that was nurtured decades ago in his university career. We benefit, as his eager students did so long ago, from his lucid style and his gift for rendering the complex understandable but not simplistic. These qualities attracted many to his lectures, even Protestant and Orthodox students in an era when such cross-pollination rarely if ever occurred.

We also encounter the same commitment that he demonstrated in his academic career to drawing attention to the truth of the faith as it is grounded in Scripture and the early Church Fathers. In a way that shows he is deeply aware of history, Pope Benedict draws from every well available, confident in the truth to be found there.

Finally, we will find Pope Benedict being forthright about the fruits of the Second Vatican Council, that event so crucial to the Church's history and with which he was so intimately involved. Joseph Ratzinger was positive about the Second Vatican Council. He has stated repeatedly that alongside the riches of preconciliar spirituality, devotion, and liturgical life, there lurked a certain closing off of the theological process, which had become dry and cut off from the richness of Scripture and patristic writers. He has questioned an approach to moral theology that resulted in legalistic thinking. He supported the council's emphasis on openness in these areas and a return to the premedieval sources of Catholic teaching and life, which was one important stated aim of the council.

However, very soon after the end of the council—and in some respects, even before—Joseph Ratzinger became disturbed by certain tendencies he observed among theologians, clergy, and other Church leaders. There was a definite sense of iconoclasm in the air, a feeling that everything in the Church—even the most fundamental teachings—was up for grabs. He also disagreed with a prevailing notion that the Church and its teachings and practices were realities that were human-centered rather than God-centered, that could and should be re-created according to the perceived needs of the present moment, and that "experts"—theologians and liturgists—were better suited to construct Catholic life than the slow action of the Holy Spirit working through the complexities and mysteries of human life and culture over the centuries.

So when we read Pope Benedict today, although he does not directly address the Second Vatican Council very frequently, it is helpful to keep in mind that he is bringing many experiences of life before, during, and after the council into his observations. This is true, for example, when he calls us to remember the true purpose of liturgy as offering worship to God rather than affirming ourselves, or when he says that a theologian's function is to serve the truth he or she discovers in Revelation and Tradition rather than creating something new and popular. This is also true when he says that devotions and prayers of the past can still speak to us since "What earlier generations held as sacred, remains sacred and great for us too, and it cannot be all of a sudden entirely forbidden or even considered harmful."[8]

Serving the Church

In 1977 Joseph Ratzinger's world changed dramatically. In March of that year, he was appointed archbishop of Munich, and shortly after, in June, elevated to cardinal.

Just four years later, Pope John Paul II, who had first met Ratzinger during the Second Vatican Council in Rome, asked him to return to Rome and serve as prefect of the Congregation for the Doctrine of the Faith. After prayer and discernment, Cardinal Ratzinger accepted the appointment.

The Congregation for the Doctrine of the Faith is the office in the Roman Curia responsible for safeguarding the teachings of the Church. The office examines publications to be used in Catholic institutions for the purpose of instruction. It mediates theological controversies and oversees the work of various other bodies charged with exploring theological ideas, such as the International Theological Commission. It produces various types of documents on theological matters and assists the pope in the composition of teaching documents such as encyclicals. The *Catechism of the Catholic Church*, published in 1992, is the fruit of the work of this congregation.

As prefect of the CDF, as it is called, Cardinal Ratzinger held ultimate responsibility for all of this work. Given all we have explored about his past, it is not surprising to learn that he had a profound sense of his office—and indeed any teaching office in the Church—as one centered on protecting, preserving, and effectively proclaiming the truths of the Catholic faith to the world.

In his twenty-six years with the CDF, Cardinal Ratzinger was immersed, every day, in the difficulties and obstacles that the Church faces in effectively sharing the Good News with the world. That might even be a good way to describe the central role of this congregation: to support and guide the Church's ministers and teachers in bringing Christ into the modern world. Theologians face challenges in translating ancient modes of thinking and speaking into modern idioms, and attempts at translation can sometimes slide into accommodation, leaving the core of the gospel obscured or even lost. When that happens, the congregation must step in so that those who need to hear this gospel are not left adrift.

As we read Pope Benedict's words in the next few chapters, we will encounter his concern to protect and preserve the faith. Pope Benedict is a theologian himself, so he obviously values the role of the theologian in the Church, yet he never shies from offering caution and correction. He has experienced a friendship with Christ that has sustained him through decades, and he wants us to experience that friendship as well, so he warns us of the ways in which earthly powers and even aspects of Church life can get in the way. And as we go through our own decades of life, he calls us to open our eyes to the many rich and surprising ways that Jesus comes to meet us.

CHAPTER TWO

MEETING OURSELVES

Being Christian is not the result of an ethical choice or a lofty idea, but the encounter with an event, a person, which gives life a new horizon and a decisive direction.[9]

We have taken some time to place Pope Benedict in context. Now what about us? What's our context?

Pope Benedict is thoroughly focused on Christ and understands his own ministry as the answer to a call from God to do what he can to help the rest of us embrace our own calling: to know and love Christ.

But why is this even an issue, especially among those who call themselves Christians? Isn't that what we're all about? Do we really need further clarification, encouragement, or inspiration about Jesus?

I cannot speak for you or anyone else, but I do know, quite honestly, that for me, listening to what Pope Benedict has to say about the role of Jesus in the life of a Christian disciple has been bracing, eye-opening, and a little distressing—especially as I consider my own relationship with Jesus and the assumptions informing so much of what I believe.

Every person is different, of course, but it's not unreasonable to suggest that a great many of us do share certain assumptions about the nature of Christian life and belief, specific to this time and place in which we live. It might be easier to understand this concept by looking at past eras.

In medieval Christianity, for example, many varieties of spirituality flourished, with individuals and movements emphasizing different aspects of faith. But even with this variety, certain assumptions were commonly held: for example, that an individual believer would find religious truth, not primarily through searching his or her own heart and experience, but by listening to and obeying religious authorities.

We may not be aware of the assumptions informing our twenty-first century belief. They may hold varying degrees of influence over our thinking. But they are indeed present, part of the spiritual air we breathe:

- Faith is primarily private and subjective. It is good to have "faith," but less important is what you have faith *in*.

- One's spiritual journey is about finding an internal space of emotional affirmation and fulfillment.

- One's spiritual journey is also about being enabled and empowered to succeed, achieve, and accomplish.

- A good faith community is one that helps you discover who you really are and helps you become the best, most fulfilled person you can be.

- Faith in Jesus Christ means essentially following him as a teacher and model.

- There have been many wise teachers in history, but we follow Jesus because we believe he had a special relationship with God, because he was the wisest teacher, and because he sacrificed his life on the cross out of love. However, other ways of listening to and learning about the spiritual journey tell us just as much about God as the Christian story, just on a slightly different path, leading to the same essential place.

- We can learn about Jesus from the Bible and from the Church's teachings, but they are both of limited value because of the distance between those sources and the present day, as well as the biases of those who have remembered and recorded.

- What is more important than seeking an objective, trustworthy account of who Jesus is and what he wants of us today is to rely on what we discern about him in our own hearts, rooted in our own experiences.

You might agree with all of the above, some, or none. But I think it's hard to deny that many Christians today in the twenty-first century frame their spiritual lives around the basic assumptions that following Jesus' teachings is a good, helpful way to live and that "church" is the place where we gather with like-minded believers to celebrate this way of living. It is mostly a private matter, with few, if any, implications beyond the confines of my own thinking and actions.

But is this the gospel?

Is this why the apostles scattered to the four corners of the known world and each died a martyr's death?

Is this the gospel about which Paul wrote, "Woe to me if I do not proclaim [it]!" (1 Corinthians 9:16)?

I'm offering these thoughts, not for the purpose of condemning us (notice the first-person plural!), but rather as an invitation to be honest about what we really believe. If we can't do that, then not much of what Pope Benedict has to say to us about Jesus will make sense, and much of it will either confuse or even offend us.

In a year-end speech to the Roman Curia in 2007, Pope Benedict effectively summarized everything we are going to explore in the rest of this book. It is worth pondering and contrasting his words with our own assumptions about who Jesus is, how he can be known, where he is to be reliably found today, and the impact that faith has on us and the world:

> Being disciples of Christ—what does this mean? Well, in the first place it means being able to recognize him. How does this happen? It is an invitation to listen to him just as he speaks to us in the text of Sacred Scripture, as he addresses us and comes to meet us in the common prayer of the Church, in the sacraments, and in the witness of the saints. One can never know Christ only theoretically. With great teaching one can know everything about the Sacred Scriptures without ever having met him. Journeying with him is an integral part of knowing him, of entering his sentiments, as the Letter to the Philippians (2:5) says. Paul briefly describes these sentiments: having the same love, being of the same mind (*sýmpsychoi*), being in full accord, doing nothing out of rivalry and

boastfulness, each one not only focusing on his or her own interests but also on those of others (2:2-4). Catechesis can never be merely the instruction of the mind; it must always also become a practice of communion of life with Christ, an exercise in humility, justice, and love. Only in this way do we walk with Jesus Christ on his path; only in this way are the eyes of our hearts opened; only in this way do we learn to understand Scripture and to meet him. The encounter with Jesus Christ requires listening, requires a response in prayer and in putting into practice what he tells us. By getting to know Christ, we come to know God, and it is only by starting from God that we understand man and the world, a world that would otherwise remain a nonsensical question.[10]

What we see first of all is that faith is not about ideas or even about "following the teachings of Christ." It is about being in an intimate relationship with him and letting him be the voice and presence that moves our hearts.

We know this, or at least we say we do. But even so, there remains a cloud of skepticism or even suspicion about our faith lives. The assumptions I listed above all add up to one big, overbearing cloud: we wonder if any of what we say we know or feel about Jesus is real. Part of this is rooted in our humanity and in the doubt inherent in the distance between the divine and the human, doubt about which the pope has written quite a bit. In fact, much of the first section of *Introduction to Christianity* explores the nature of doubt in a sympathetic way.

But even beyond that, our contemporary sensibilities plant more seeds of doubt and skepticism in our mind. It seems as if every word of Scripture is questioned, even by Christian scholars. The Church changes, and leaders in the Church even commit serious sin in the Church's name. There are so many different points of view and religious paths in the world, filled with apparently perfectly happy people.

As I question my own personal, existential distance from God and the apparent shortcomings of the texts and institutions that are supposed to bridge that gap, how can I even believe that meeting Jesus—the real Jesus—is possible?

This is really one of the most fundamental questions that Pope Benedict addresses, directly and indirectly. What he repeatedly assures us is that it is indeed possible for us to meet and be in relationship with the real Jesus.

He speaks often about listening to Jesus through his body, the Church, through the word of God, and through the liturgical life of the Church. Our first instinct might be to see this in a negative way, as if he is trying to tell us that the ways in which we can meet Jesus are limited and must be controlled. But this is truly the opposite of the pope's intention. He wants us to see all of this, not as places with walls and rules, but as gifts through which Jesus really and truly comes to meet us. We can trust them, and we can trust him.

We *can* know Christ. It is possible. It is not all in our heads or dreams. It is not a story we tell ourselves over and over so that we can feel some degree of comfort or so that we have the energy to get up tomorrow and live our best life. He promised to be with us always, and he is.

Pope Benedict invites us to recognize that this faith we profess may not be about what we thought it was. It's not about obligations and rules. It's not about fitting in culturally or socially.

It's not about controlling our kids' behavior. It's not about living by some helpful ideas that may be good for you, but not so great for me.

It's about the reality of Jesus Christ, living now, inviting you and me into ever-deepening friendship with him, and not just for our own individual sake, but for the sake of the whole world he has come to redeem. When we are baptized and brought into the life of Christ, we become part of an enormous, astounding, cosmic reality.

Sounds rather exciting. And to Pope Benedict it is, for there is one word he uses quite frequently when he writes about the life of a disciple—"adventure."

He writes of the apostles:

This is how the apostles' adventure began, as an encounter of people who are open to one another. For the disciples, it was the beginning of a direct acquaintance with the Teacher, seeing where he was staying and starting to get to know him. Indeed, they were not to proclaim an idea, but to witness to a person.[11]

Of Peter specifically:

He accepted this surprising call, he let himself be involved in this great adventure: he was generous; he recognized his limits but believed in the one who was calling him and followed the dream of his heart. He said "yes," a courageous and generous "yes," and became a disciple of Jesus.[12]

Of St. Augustine of Hippo:

Faith in Christ brought all Augustine's seeking to fulfillment, but fulfillment in the sense that he always remained
on the way. Indeed, he tells us: even in eternity our seeking
will not be completed, it will be an eternal adventure, the
discovery of new greatness, new beauty.[13]

And what about us now? Is discipleship still an adventure?
Benedict invites us to see it that way. When speaking to young
people—as he does here in an off-the-cuff, question-and-answer
session—he never hesitates to use the language of adventure.
But no matter what our age, this language can speak to us, if
we allow it to:

To return to the question, I think it is important to be attentive to the Lord's gestures on our journey. He speaks to us
through events, through people, through encounters: it is
necessary to be attentive to all of this.

Then, a second point: it is necessary to enter into real
friendship with Jesus in a personal relationship with him
and not to know who Jesus is only from others or from
books, but to live an ever deeper personal relationship
with Jesus, where we can begin to understand what he is
asking of us.

And then, the awareness of what I am, of my possibilities: on the one hand, courage, and on the other, humility, trust, and openness, with the help also of friends, of

Church authority, and also of priests, of families: what does the Lord want of me?

Of course, this is always a great adventure, but life can be successful only if we have the courage to be adventurous, trusting that the Lord will never leave me alone, that the Lord will go with me and help me.[14]

CHAPTER THREE

MEETING JESUS IN THE MEANING OF LIFE

*Darkness, at times, can seem comfortable. I can hide,
and spend my life asleep. Yet we are not called to darkness,
but to light.*[15]

Why are you here?

Not just, why are you wherever you happen to be, reading this book on this particular day? But why are you—the individual you are—on this earth? Why do you exist? Why do you *not* exist?

What's your purpose? What is going to bring you the most joy, peace, and satisfaction in the blip of time you've got here with the rest of us before you head on?

There may be times—huge chunks of time, even years—during which we think we can dismiss this question, or that the answer seems too obvious for comment. Perhaps life keeps us too busy to think about it, or perhaps we purposefully avoid it. But most of us have to face the question at some point, because life has a habit of forcing us to do so.

Several years ago, I was sitting in the dentist's office, waiting for a routine appointment. For some reason that day, I was thinking about life's meaning and faith and such matters and was at a point of throwing up my hands, in a relatively cheerful kind of way, at the complexity of it all. Maybe it *didn't* all need to be so complex. Maybe I should stop worrying, be happy, live and let live, and not stress so much about the big questions. Maybe I shouldn't even worry so much about the spiritual stuff, with all of those hints of "sacrifice." Life is good. Why not enjoy it?

Then a woman rushed in, announced herself at the reception desk, and was told that her appointment was actually the following week.

Frazzled, she breathlessly said, in a torrent of words, "Oh, I'm sorry. I was nine months pregnant, then last week the baby just died. I'm not really thinking straight."

And she rushed out.

Like a heavy, damp cloud, the big picture rushed back in, and the questions reasserted themselves again, loudly, like an unexpected late summer storm.

No Accidents

When we think about life's meaning, it comes to us in (at least) two different ways. First, like the philosophers, we consider the general meaning of existence—why things exist, what the shape and nature of reality reveal about meaning, and so on.

We also consider, more urgently, the reason for our own personal existence instead of nonexistence. Why did that random sperm and egg meet at that particular moment to create me? What if they hadn't? The fact that even the very beginnings of our existence seem so contingent on so many variables—on whether or not our parents ever met, or whether or not they were feeling romantic at that moment—can stop us in our tracks. If the difference between my existence and nonexistence was an extra glass of wine or an argument finally resolved, what meaning can that existence actually have?

Mixed up with that type of meaning is the question of purpose. I'm here (however *that* happened) . . . so now what? Happiness, pleasure, satisfaction, sacrifice, accomplishment, contentment . . . is it about that? Or is it about completely forgetting my own needs and pouring out every gram of my soul for others? Is suffering a sure sign that my life is meaningless—or most meaning*ful?*

The world gives plenty of answers.

During his pontificate, Pope Benedict has alluded to these answers many times. Some might assume that a man in his eighties who worked within the confines of the Roman Curia for decades would have little insight into the shape of the contemporary search for meaning, but that is not true. Pope Benedict is a close observer and a careful listener, profoundly interested in how human beings encounter God, not just in general, but in this particular cultural circumstance in which we find ourselves, because Curia or not, those are the circumstances in which he lives and ministers as well.

Pope Benedict has, indeed, listened to modern men and women. He was a parish priest and a bishop; he hears confessions; as prefect of the CDF, he read the files of troubled clergy for decades; and throughout his whole career, he has interacted generously and open-mindedly with nonbelievers. He knows the obstacles, the temptations, and the barriers this world throws up, not only to God, but to the possibility of ultimate meaning and transcendence in general. He also seems, in a personal way, very familiar with doubt—the question of doubt reappears often in his writings and comprises a large section of the first part of his *Introduction to Christianity.*

But he also knows that this world is not so different than it always has been, despite our tendency to think so. The wheels may spin faster, on cleaner streets, but human beings still yearn, life still confounds, and Jesus still waits for us, ready for us at the moment we decide that we are ready for him.

The Universe

We're not going to take the time to rehearse the entire history of scientific thought since the Renaissance and Enlightenment, because we're all conversant with the outline: as human knowledge about the material forces of the universe has expanded, the transcendent has been pushed out.

Contemporary human beings live in a confusing mix. We are so aware of those material forces but still just as aware of the reality of what lives in our own hearts. Certainly we are collections of cells, and we do spin on a planet, in a universe governed by various laws, and perhaps we even evolved from lower life forms, but really . . . is that all there is to us?

And if there really is more, is it just a matter of my own individual experience and opinion, as the world suggests, unique to me, which means that even as my own personal set of meanings lives with me, it will also die with me? Is there an objective, lasting ground to *anything about my life?*

One of the consequences of a world from which God has been marginalized or ejected is that humans then believe themselves to be self-sufficient—a problem that Pope Benedict often addresses. If the universe does not need God, a rational creating Mind, that must mean that the rational products of this universe do not need

God either. Everything that exists, everything that we create—our culture, our social systems, our moral systems, our political and civic organizations—is better off without God.

To believe in a creator God, however, doesn't mean we have to question the value or necessity of science or secular fields of study, or even randomness, chance, or chaos, all of which seem to play a role in the cosmos. Instead, it means placing explanations of the physical aspects of the world in their proper context:

> It is not the elemental spirits of the universe, the laws of matter, which ultimately govern the world and mankind, but a personal God governs the stars, that is, the universe; it is not the laws of matter and of evolution that have the final say, but reason, will, love—a Person. And if we know this Person and he knows us, then truly the inexorable power of material elements no longer has the last word; we are not slaves of the universe and of its laws, we are free. In ancient times, honest enquiring minds were aware of this. Heaven is not empty. Life is not a simple product of laws and the randomness of matter, but within everything and at the same time above everything, there is a personal will, there is a Spirit who in Jesus has revealed himself as Love.[16]

Still, we might ask, as I did on that morning in the dentist's office, so what? Isn't it all good? What's the harm in letting the secular dominate in the realms of science, culture, society, and politics, and saving God for the privacy of my own heart?

Well, we might answer with another question. How's that working out for us so far?

Pope Benedict has an idea, as he expressed it here to young people in Cologne at World Youth Day in 2005, just months after his election:

In the last century, we experienced revolutions with a common program—expecting nothing more from God, they assumed total responsibility for the cause of the world in order to change it. And this, as we saw, meant that a human and partial point of view was always taken as an absolute guiding principle. Absolutizing what is not absolute but relative is called totalitarianism. It does not liberate man, but takes away his dignity and enslaves him.[17]

What Pope Benedict points out is also an ancient observation: that when human powers establish themselves as the primary arbiters of meaning and freedom and turn from the transcendent, they place themselves in the role of the transcendent and the absolute, and often end up demanding absolute authority and submission.

The examples from past and present of authoritarian regimes are obvious. But frequently, Pope Benedict calls us to be more discerning so that we realize how even in democratic, capitalist societies, earthly powers can claim absolute authority. Scientific and medical authorities embark on paths that objectify human beings and even have the power to destroy creation, but refuse accountability on the basis of their authority. A commercial culture works hard to impose its own glittering, fast-moving kind of "authoritarian" regime in which values are certainly imposed with as much force as any political regime, as the pope indicated at another World Youth Day, in Sydney, in 2008:

Dear friends, life is not governed by chance; it is not random. Your very existence has been willed by God, blessed and given a purpose (cf. Genesis 1:28)! Life is not just a succession of events or experiences, helpful though many of them are. It is a search for the true, the good, and the beautiful. It is to this end that we make our choices; it is for this that we exercise our freedom; it is in this—in truth, in goodness, and in beauty—that we find happiness and joy. Do not be fooled by those who see you as just another consumer in a market of undifferentiated possibilities, where choice itself becomes the good, novelty usurps beauty, and subjective experience displaces truth.[18]

We all know what totalitarian, atheistic regimes do to human life. We know the wreckage of devalued human life produced by a profit- and achievement-seeking, God-forgetting culture.

Therefore, we ourselves have this very deep certainty that Christ is the answer and that without the concrete God, the God with the face of Christ, the world destroys itself; and there is growing evidence that a closed rationalism, which thinks that human beings can rebuild the world better on their own, is not true. On the contrary, without the restraint of the true God, human beings destroy themselves. We see this with our own eyes.[19]

Pope Benedict also has some observations on how we as individuals fare in a world that tells us that God doesn't matter, that there is no inherent meaning, and that maybe we don't matter either. Here is what he said in the very first homily he gave as pope, at his own installation Mass:

> The pastor must be inspired by Christ's holy zeal: for him it is not a matter of indifference that so many people are living in the desert. And there are so many kinds of desert. There is the desert of poverty, the desert of hunger and thirst, the desert of abandonment, of loneliness, of destroyed love. There is the desert of God's darkness, the emptiness of souls no longer aware of their dignity or the goal of human life. The external deserts in the world are growing, because the internal deserts have become so vast. Therefore the earth's treasures no longer serve to build God's garden for all to live in, but they have been made to serve the powers of exploitation and destruction.[20]

And here is what he has to say in other contexts:

> The world needs this renewal! In so many of our societies, side by side with material prosperity, a spiritual desert is spreading: an interior emptiness, an unnamed fear, a quiet sense of despair. How many of our contemporaries have built broken and empty cisterns (cf. Jeremiah 2:13) in a desperate search for meaning—the ultimate meaning that only love can give?[21]

Yes, man needs transcendence. God alone suffices, Teresa of Ávila said. If God is absent, man must seek by himself to go beyond the world's boundaries, to open before him the boundless space for which he was created. Drugs then become, as it were, a need for him. Yet he very soon discovers that they are an unending illusion—one might say, a trick the devil plays on man.[22]

If we look at today's world where God is absent, we cannot but note that it is also dominated by fears and uncertainties: is it good to be a person or not? Is it good to be alive or not? Is it truly a good to exist? Or might everything be negative? And they really live in a dark world; they need anaesthetics to be able to live.[23]

It is probably not too difficult to personalize these insights. Even those of us who might characterize our religious faith as "strong" toss up idols in the corner of our lives. We may even offer "sacrifices" to these idols—idols not constructed of stone, but of wishes, hopes, and goals. When I put the treasure of my intellect and spirit in the hope and yes, the faith, that my happiness is dependent on something other than God, then I've offered a bit of sacrifice to an idol. And this can be anything. It can be great, massive things, or it can be tiny things—if my happiness is dependent on my weight, if my happiness is dependent on my professional achievement, if my happiness is dependent on my children's achievement—and in the end, even if my happiness is dependent on my spouse's love for me.

I've idolized when I've sought the transcendent in what is not transcendent. As St. Augustine observed seventeen hundred years ago, "Our hearts are restless until they rest in thee, O Lord." We are made for God, made to rest in God. We yearn for the lasting, never-failing love and rock-solid truth that only God can give us.

And if we think about it, we place an unfair burden on other people when we make our own happiness dependent on their love for us or their ability to please us. We are, in effect, putting that person in the place of God in our lives.

This is an important element of Pope Benedict's encyclical *Spe Salvi* (Saved in Hope):

In some way we want life itself, true life, untouched even by death; yet at the same time we do not know the thing toward which we feel driven. We cannot stop reaching out for it, and yet we know that all we can experience or accomplish is not what we yearn for. This unknown "thing" is the true "hope" which drives us, and at the same time the fact that it is unknown is the cause of all forms of despair and also of all efforts, whether positive or destructive, directed toward worldly authenticity and human authenticity. . . .

Let us summarize what has emerged so far in the course of our reflections. Day by day, man experiences many greater or lesser hopes, different in kind according to the different periods of his life. Sometimes one of these hopes may appear to be totally satisfying without any need for other hopes. Young people can have the hope of a great and fully satisfying love; the hope of a certain position in their profession, or of some success that will prove decisive for the rest of their lives. When these hopes are fulfilled, however, it becomes clear that they were not, in reality, the whole. It becomes evident that man has need of a hope that goes further. It becomes clear that only something infinite will suffice for him, something that will always be more than he can ever attain.[24]

So we hope, but do we even know what it is we are hoping for? One of Pope Benedict's recurring themes is the reality of how our vision and hearing are impaired, how our yearnings, which are really all for God in the end, are misdirected, and how life—both in general and contemporary life in particular—blinds us to the real object of our yearning:

> In the course of human history, a thick layer of dirt has covered God's good creation, which makes it difficult if not impossible to perceive in it the Creator's reflection, although the knowledge of the Creator's existence is reawakened within us ever anew, as it were, spontaneously, at the sight of a sunset over the sea, on an excursion to the mountains, or before a flower that has just bloomed.[25]

There is not only a physical deafness which largely cuts people off from social life; there is also a "hardness of hearing" where God is concerned, and this is something from which we particularly suffer in our own time. Put simply, we are no longer able to hear God—there are too many different frequencies filling our ears. What is said about God strikes us as prescientific, no longer suited to our age. Along with this hardness of hearing or outright deafness where God is concerned, we naturally lose our ability to speak with him and to him. And so we end up losing a decisive capacity for perception. We risk losing our inner senses. This weakening of our capacity for perception drastically and dangerously curtails the range of our relationship with reality in general. The horizon of our life is disturbingly foreshortened.[26]

How true this is! We are made for God, for the transcendent, for eternal life, but our sensitivity to that reality has been damaged. It has been damaged, as it has for all humanity, by sin. But in this age, it is also damaged by the world in which we live and which we allow to affect us: a world that teaches us, forms us, and sometimes even forces us to live as if the transcendent and God were nonexistent, were not a part of the reality that surrounds us. And if we're unaware of the existence of something, we never think about it; it doesn't enter our consciousness or our decision making. That's the dynamic energizing so much of the idol-construction in our lives.

What is the answer for this searching, yearning world? Where is true freedom to be found?

Jesus.

Pope Benedict's invitation is simple:

Confronted with these deeper questions concerning the origin and destiny of mankind, Christianity proposes Jesus of Nazareth.[27]

Christianity "proposes Jesus of Nazareth" to the world—and to you and me.

At the heart of all of our searching and striving is the hope that in the end, what we have been about is True, and what we have lived is Love, and that what we have left is Beauty, and that all of these things will last forever.

You may not call it God, and you might be trying to find those things, half-blind, fully deaf, grappling in the muck of sin, but that is what you were made for, and that is what you are looking for.

Over and over again, in his preaching and teaching, Pope Benedict invites each of us to examine our search and honestly consider where our blind spots are, and then simply turn to Jesus and listen:

> But the Creator Spirit comes to our aid. He has entered history and speaks to us in a new way. In Jesus Christ, God himself was made man and allowed us, so to speak, to cast a glance at the intimacy of God himself.
>
> And there we see something totally unexpected: in God, an "I" and a "You" exist. The mysterious God is not infinite loneliness; he is an event of love. If by gazing at creation we think we can glimpse the Creator Spirit, God himself, rather like creative mathematics, like a force that shapes the laws of the world and their order, but then, even, also like beauty—now we come to realize: the Creator Spirit has a heart. He is Love.
>
> . . . Yet Jesus did not only let us see into God's intimacy; with him, God also emerged, as it were, from his intimacy and came to meet us. This happened especially in his life, passion, death, and resurrection; in his words.[28]

Here we encounter, and not for the last time, the essence of Pope Benedict's Christology. It will come to us again and again.

In Jesus, God and humanity meet. In Jesus, we meet God; in Jesus, God meets us. Jesus, fully human and divine, is the One who not only teaches us how to be human and not only teaches us about God, but, in his divine presence in our world and in our own lives, *saves* us. He rescues us from sin, from death; he opens our eyes and ears so that we can be freed from the death-dealing snares of the world and be opened to the horizons that God has established for us—which are the horizons of eternal, unending love and truth:

> Jesus Christ is the Personified Truth who attracts the world to himself. The light that shines out from Jesus is the splendor of the truth. Every other truth is a fragment of the Truth that he is, and refers to him.
>
> Jesus is the Pole Star of human freedom: without him, it loses its sense of direction, for without the knowledge of the truth, freedom degenerates, becomes isolated, and is reduced to sterile arbitration. With him, freedom is rediscovered; it is recognized to have been created for our good and is expressed in charitable actions and behavior.
>
> . . . And nothing succeeds as well as love for the truth in impelling the human mind toward unexplored horizons. Jesus Christ, who is the fullness of the truth, draws to himself the heart of each person, enlarges it, and fills it with joy. Indeed, truth alone can take possession of the mind and make it rejoice to the full.

It is this joy that increases the dimensions of the human heart, lifting it anew from the narrowness of selfishness and rendering it capable of authentic love. It is the experience of this joy that moves and attracts the human person to free adoration, not to servile prostration but to bow with heartfelt respect before the Truth he has encountered.[29]

The point is this: we are all made to seek the eternal, for God has made us that way. Why? Because he wants us to seek *him*.

In Jesus, we have the amazing gift of God, offering himself to us—really offering, on a cross—to both *show* us what we are really meant for and, by breaking down the barriers of sin and death and dwelling with us, *taking us* to that end, which is the love, truth, beauty, and eternal life that we all yearn for. He shows the way. He *is* the way.

Our light, our truth, our goal, our fulfillment, our life—all this is not a religious doctrine but a person: Jesus Christ. Over and above any ability of our own to seek and to desire God, we ourselves were already sought and desired, and indeed, found and redeemed by him! The gaze of people of every time and nation, of all the philosophies, religions, and cultures, ultimately encounters the wide-open eyes of the crucified and risen Son of God; his open heart is the fullness of love. The eyes of Christ are the eyes of a loving God. The image of the crucified Lord . . . shows that this gaze is turned to every man and woman. The Lord, in truth, looks into the hearts of each of us.[30]

Dear friends, truth is not an imposition. Nor is it simply a set of rules. It is a discovery of the One who never fails us; the One whom we can always trust. In seeking truth we come to live by belief, because ultimately truth is a person: Jesus Christ.[31]

CHAPTER FOUR

MEETING JESUS
IN THE SCRIPTURES

We must always look for the Word within the words.[32]

We have met Jesus. We suspect—or even affirm—that he is what he says he is: the Way, the Truth, and the Life. We confront the image of him crucified, and it won't leave us. We read what he says about being free from burdens, the possibility of eternal life, and God's care for us when we are lost. We are, as Pope Benedict wrote of St. Peter, "fascinated" by Jesus.

Now what?

The figure of Jesus Christ beckons and intrigues us. We're drawn to learn more about him, so it makes sense that we turn to the source: the Bible.

It does, indeed, make perfect sense to turn to the Scriptures as we seek to know Jesus. In fact, as St. Jerome says, it makes no sense to claim to know Jesus *without* the Scriptures: "He who is ignorant of the Scriptures is ignorant of Christ."

Pope Benedict said in a speech in 2008:

How can one love, how can one enter into friendship with someone unknown? Knowledge is an incentive to love, and love stimulates knowledge. This is how it is with Christ too.

To find love with Christ, to truly find him as the companion of our lives, we must first of all be acquainted with him.

The two disciples who followed him after hearing the words of John the Baptist and asked him timidly, "Rabbi, where are you staying?" wanted to know him better. It was Jesus himself, talking to his disciples, who made the distinction: "Who do people say that I am?"—referring to those who knew him from afar, so to speak, by hearsay, and "Who do you say that I am?"—referring to those who knew him personally, having lived with him and having truly penetrated his private life, to the point of witnessing his prayer, his dialogue with the Father. Thus, it is also important for us not to reduce ourselves merely to the superficiality of the many who have heard something about him—that he was an important figure, etc.—but to enter into a personal relationship to know him truly. And this demands knowledge of Scripture, especially of the gospels where the Lord speaks to us.[33]

But for many of us, finding and getting to know Jesus through the Scriptures is really not as simple as it sounds. We may be intimidated by the prospect of reading the Bible, since we have never really studied it. We may, unfortunately, think of Scripture reading and study as something for Protestants, not Catholics.

We may also be working within some particularly modern paradigms of viewing the Bible, paradigms that are of great interest to Pope Benedict and that he addresses frequently in his catechesis. In short, are we too studious about the Bible—and not prayerful enough?

For a very long time, both as a student and teacher of Scripture in Catholic schools and parishes, I thought I understood the proper, most fruitful way to approach the Bible: to do what the Scripture scholars do.

And what do Scripture scholars do? They use various methodologies to exegete—closely study—the Scriptures. They look at history, background, linguistic issues, cultural issues, and social setting. They examine and compare texts and manuscripts. They do all kinds of worthy, important, and enlightening things.

When I studied the Bible as a high school freshman in the late 1970s, my textbooks and teachers took this same approach, starting right off the bat with Genesis. We were told that scholars had established that there were four basic strands of writing running through the book, and indeed, the entire Pentateuch. They were known by their initials as J, E, P, and D—standing for Jahwist, Eloihist, Priestly, and Deuteronomist traditions.

We were guided through the text of Genesis with this at the forefront: pick out the sections that scholars believe emerged from the Jahwist tradition and compare them to those written that came from the Priestly. See how they are different. See how they fit together—or don't. Make a chart about J, E, P, and D. Test on Monday.

The same approach was taken with the New Testament, especially the gospels. We were taught that scholars knew that Mark had been written first, Matthew and Luke written later, depending on each other as well as a mysterious document called "Q," and John came last—much later—because it had the most developed and exalted view of Christ. This was all established; it was all really beyond question.

So we read the gospels, comparing the texts of the beatitudes, the infancy narratives, the Lord's prayers, various parables and miracles, the passion and resurrection of Jesus. Again, as we had with the Old Testament, we compared and contrasted, focusing our energies on pulling out the differences in the various versions and pondering those differences. We also concentrated on what we were told were the intended audiences of each of the gospel writers and were asked to think about the implications and meaning of how Matthew or Luke arranged this story or changed the way Jesus spoke. Along the way we might have encountered assertions about how much of Jesus' reported words scholars believe he actually uttered himself. What it usually came down to was what we now call the Lord's Prayer and "Abba."

When I started teaching, I used the available textbooks, which were all written with this scholarly, dissecting approach—for ninth graders!—although as time went on, I began to suspect that this wasn't quite cutting it. Were my students really getting to know Jesus this way? Were they being encouraged to take the word of God more seriously—or less?

And then, years later, I started exploring contemporary biblical studies again.

And what did I discover?

JEPD? Maybe, maybe not. Some scholars were disputing it. Marcan priority? Not so fast, some scholars were saying. There's good evidence that Matthew could have come first. Q? Such a thing could have existed, but, I discovered, there's a whole branch of New Testament scholarship that argues, with good evidence, that it might not, and that perhaps the points of agreement between Matthew and Luke are due to mutual dependence, not dependence on a mysterious third text. John being way late and last? Some scholars argue that John might be closer to the composition of the synoptics than we thought, and that, if we read closely, the supposed "low" Christology of Mark perhaps isn't so low after all.

The point was, not only that what I had been presented as, well, "gospel" truths about biblical composition and transmission were far from infallible, but also that using the approach of a scholar, perhaps I was missing something important.

Where was Christ?

Assumptions

Pope Benedict is a theologian, not a professional Scripture scholar, but from the beginning of his career, his work has been deeply rooted in Scripture. In fact, as you might recall from our biographical chapter, one of the elements that set him apart as a teacher and young theologian from other Catholic scholars was the fact that his lectures and writings were like tapestries woven from threads of Scripture, history, and the early Church Fathers, rather than syllogisms or dry assertions about abstract truth.

He has been a close observer of biblical scholarship, and of course, as prefect of the CDF, oversaw the work of the Pontifical Biblical Commission. He has never hesitated to both affirm the importance of the work of exegetes but also point out the limits of the scholarly approach, especially in the modern age when the "scientific" approach—one divorced from theology—has dominated the academic field, even among professing Christians:

Our exegesis has progressed by leaps and bounds. We truly know a great deal about the development of texts, the subdivision of sources, etc., we know what words would have meant at that time. . . . But we are increasingly seeing that if historical and critical exegesis remains solely historical and critical, it refers the Word to the past, it makes it a Word of those times, a Word which basically says nothing to us at all; and we see that the Word is fragmented, precisely because it is broken up into a multitude of different sources.[34]

And:

This should be said now, critically, with regard to a certain part of modern exegesis that thinks it has understood everything and that, therefore, after the interpretation it has worked out, there is nothing left to say about it. This is not true. The Word is always greater than the exegesis of the Fathers and critical exegesis because even this comprehends only a part, indeed, a minimal part. The Word is always greater; this is our immense consolation. And on the one hand, it is lovely to know that one has only understood a little. It is lovely to know that there is still an inexhaustible treasure and that every new generation will rediscover new treasures and journey on with the greatness of the Word of God that is always before us, guides us, and is ever greater. One should read the Scriptures with an awareness of this.[35]

Here Pope Benedict reminds us of two points regarding professional biblical exegesis: first, that it is limited to treating its subject as texts from the past, not a living word, and second, that when we focus our attention solely on academic criticism as a way into the text, we think that the answers scholars provide are sufficient to a complete understanding.

In this context, St. Augustine recalls the scribes and Pharisees who were consulted by Herod when the Magi arrived. Herod wants to know where the Savior of the world would be born. They know it, they give the correct answer: in Bethlehem. They are great specialists who know everything. However they do not see reality, they do not know the Savior. St. Augustine says: they are signs on the road for others, but they themselves do not move. This is a great danger as well in our reading of Scripture: we stop at the human words, words form the past, history of the past, and we do not discover the present in the past, the Holy Spirit who speaks to us today in the words from the past. In this way we do not enter the interior movement of the Word, which in human words conceals and which opens the divine words. Therefore, there is always a need for *exquisivi* [inquiry]. We must always look for the Word within the words.

Therefore, exegesis, the true reading of Holy Scripture, is not only a literary phenomenon, not only reading a text. It is the movement of my existence. It is moving toward the Word of God in the human words. Only by conforming ourselves to the mystery of God, to the Lord who is the Word, can we enter within the Word, can we truly find the Word of God in human words. Let us pray to the Lord that he may help us search the word, not only with our intellect, but also with our entire existence.[36]

The notes in our Bibles are useful. The study guides that point us to the meanings of original Hebrew and Greek are invaluable. But as we listen, read, and study, we can't forget that this text is different from the *Odyssey*, Plutarch's *Lives*, or even from St. Augustine's *Confessions*. As vivid as those works are, as much as they reveal about those who composed them, they are not expressions of a living word, spoken to us today, inviting our response, inviting us into a deeper, dynamic knowledge of *the Word*.

So how can we meet the living Jesus in the Scriptures?

First, we must make a decision to approach what we are reading, not as a curious outsider, but open to the presence of Christ in what we read. The Bible is not a random collection of books. The interaction of human and divine in the process of composing these texts is complicated and even mysterious, but that should be expected, shouldn't it? After all, the Word of God is speaking to us in human words—the definition of incarnation, which is a mystery.

But just as we will never learn, say, physics, if we approach the subject with hostility, suspicion, and a mind generally closed to the purpose and foundation of physics, our encounters with the word will be impoverished if we approach it closed to the presence of Christ within, to the Word guiding and binding it into a whole:

Step by step, light dawns, and the Christian can grasp what the Lord said to the disciples at Emmaus, explaining to them that it was of him that all the prophets had spoken.

The Lord unfolds to us the last re-reading; Christ is the key to all things, and only by joining the disciples on the road to Emmaus, only by walking with Christ, by reinterpreting all things in his light, with him, Crucified and Risen, do we enter into the riches and beauty of Sacred Scripture.

Therefore, I would say that the important point is not to fragment Sacred Scripture. The modern critic himself, as we now see, has enabled us to understand that it is an ongoing journey. And we can also see that it is a journey with a direction and that Christ really is its destination. By starting from Christ, we start the entire journey again and enter into the depths of the Word.

To sum up, I would say that Sacred Scripture must always be read in the light of Christ. Only in this way can we also read and understand Sacred Scripture in our own context today and be truly enlightened by it. We must understand this: Sacred Scripture is a journey with a direction. Those who know the destination can also take all those steps once again now, and can thus acquire a deeper knowledge of the mystery of Christ.[37]

Second, we must actually read and listen. Open the Scriptures ourselves, daily if we can, and immerse ourselves in that word and approach it trusting that the word is for *us*. As Pope Benedict said in a question-and-answer session with seminarians in 2007:

Now, for the first question: how can we distinguish God's voice from among the thousands of voices we hear each day in our world? I would say: God speaks with us in many different ways. He speaks through others, through friends, parents, pastors, priests. Here, the priests to whom you are entrusted, who are guiding you.

He speaks by means of the events in our life, in which we are able to discern God's touch; he speaks also through nature, creation, and he speaks, naturally and above all, through his Word, in Sacred Scripture, read in the communion of the Church and read personally in conversation with God.

It is important to read Sacred Scripture in a very personal way, and really, as St. Paul says, not as a human word or a document from the past as we read Homer or Virgil, but as God's Word, which is ever timely and speaks to me. It is important to learn to understand in a historical text, a text from the past, the living Word of God, that is, to enter into prayer and thus read Sacred Scripture as a conversation with God.[38]

A third point Pope Benedict frequently makes about reading Scripture might seem to contradict the first, as he reminds us that we do not, in fact, read alone when we read Scripture. We read with the Church.

This sensibility is rooted in the truth that the Bible is not a book delivered from heaven to millions of individuals as individuals. The Bible emerges from the experiences of the People of God and is addressed to the People of God.

We will speak more about this in the next chapter, but the seeds of that discussion can be planted here. For whatever reason—a culture that insists on making religion purely private and subjective or the influence of Protestant thinking even among Catholics on the primacy of one's individual relationship with Christ—many of us approach the Bible in this way. Then we risk forgetting that God's plan of salvation is not just about us as individuals but about redeeming *the world*. If it were, indeed, all about just individuals making their own way and discovering their own path and listening to what they can pick up, there would be no need for Church, no need for the body of Christ on earth.

Our approach to Scripture should reflect this truth, the pope reminds us:

> We should never read Scripture alone because we meet too many closed doors and could easily slip into error. The Bible has been written by the People of God and for the People of God under the inspiration of the Holy Spirit. Only in this communion with the People of God do we truly enter into the "we," into the nucleus of the truth that God himself wants to tell us. For him [St. Jerome], an authentic interpretation of the Bible must always be in harmonious accord with the faith of the Catholic Church. It does not treat of an exegesis imposed on this Book from without; the Book is really the voice of the pilgrim People of God, and only in the faith of this People are we "correctly attuned" to understand Sacred Scripture.[39]

And:

> St. Augustine often says in his homilies: I knocked on various occasions at the door of this Word until I could perceive

what God himself was saying to me. It is of paramount importance to combine this very personal reading, this personal talk with God in which I search for what the Lord is saying to me, and in addition to this personal reading, reading it in the community is very important because the living subject of Sacred Scripture is the People of God, it is the Church.

This Scripture was not simply restricted to great writers—even if the Lord always needs the person and his personal response—but it developed with people who were traveling together on the journey of the People of God and thus, their words are expressions of this journey, of this reciprocity of God's call and the human response.

Thus, the subject lives today as it lived at that time so that Scripture does not belong to the past, because its subject, the People of God inspired by this same God, is always the same, and therefore the Word is always alive in the living subject.

It is consequently important to read Sacred Scripture and experience Sacred Scripture in the communion of the Church, that is, with all the great witnesses of this Word, beginning with the first Fathers and ending with today's saints, with today's Magisterium.[40]

"Reading with the Church" involves a number of different elements:

- An internal unity with the body of Christ that involves resisting the temptation to distinguish between "spirituality" and "religion" or to view the Church as an obstacle to my spiritual life rather than its source.

- An openness to encountering the word of God, not just in my individual prayer time, but also within the liturgical life of the Church, primarily in the Liturgy of the Hours and, of course, the Mass.

Catholics sometimes forget how profoundly scriptural the liturgical life of our ancient faith is. The Liturgy of the Hours, which all are invited to pray as frequently as possible, is essentially the psalms, prayed in rotation throughout the day and the week. The Mass is rooted in Scripture, not only in the readings at daily and Sunday Mass, but in the individual prayers, antiphons, and the general shape and purpose of the Mass, which invites us to enter into the sacrifice of Jesus, with thanksgiving—all rooted in the word of God. Pope Benedict says:

Above all, it is a Word that becomes vital and alive in the liturgy. I would say, therefore, that the liturgy is the privileged place where every one of us can enter into the "we" of the sons of God, in conversation with God. This is important. The Our Father begins with the words "Our Father"; only if I am integrated into the "we" of this "Our" can I find the Father; only within this "we," which is the subject of the prayer of the Our Father, do we hear the Word of God clearly.

Thus, this seems to me most important: the liturgy is the privileged place where the Word is alive, is present, indeed, where the Word, the Logos, the Lord, speaks to us and gives himself into our hands; if we are ready to listen to the Lord in this great communion of the Church of all times, we find him. He opens the door to us little by little.[41]

So we can meet Jesus—the Word of God—in the word. He has not been disappeared by scholars or skeptics. He is there.

Meeting Jesus in the Scriptures is not a simplistic encounter. God communicates to us through human means, which are rich and complex. Besides, it is God of whom we are speaking, God whose divine simplicity is of a depth and breadth we can never fully explore. Pope Benedict is not suggesting a fundamentalist, literalist reading of Scripture, for that approach can be just as impoverished as the one that insists scholars hold the key to understanding.

We read with the trust and faith that we will meet Jesus in the word. As with any friendship, we nurture that friendship with frequent, open-minded, thoughtful encounters. I open my heart and enter the word, knowing that it is certainly given to me right now, but not only me. I am part of the People of God, part of the creation that God has redeemed, and in order to deeply meet Jesus, I must understand that he—the Word—comes for the People of whom I am a part. To hear the truth of what he has to say and drink deeply from the life offered, I should listen, not as a lone ranger exploring the corners of her own soul, but on the road with the rest of my brothers and sisters as we travel and listen together:

> We must therefore read it in communion with the living Church. The privileged place for reading and listening to the Word of God is the liturgy, in which, celebrating the Word and making Christ's body present in the Sacrament, we actualize the Word in our lives and make it present among us. We must never forget that the Word of God transcends time.

Human opinions come and go. What is very modern today will be very antiquated tomorrow. On the other hand, the Word of God is the Word of eternal life; it bears within it eternity and is valid forever. By carrying the Word of God within us, we therefore carry within us eternity, eternal life.[42]

CHAPTER FIVE

MEETING JESUS IN
THE LIFE OF THE CHURCH

With his incarnation he said: I am yours. And in baptism
he said to me: I am yours. In the Holy Eucharist, he says
ever anew: I am yours, so that we may respond: Lord, I am
yours. In the way of the Word, entering the mystery of his
incarnation, of his being among us, we want to appropriate his
being, we want to expropriate our existence, giving ourselves
to him who gave himself to us.[43]

To know Jesus Christ and to live in him—this possibility draws us. We meet him in the Scriptures, we think we hear his voice within our hearts. Yet, there are still questions that confront us.

For example, because life is complicated and the human beings who seek God are coming from every direction, every stage of life, with different personality types and needs, where do we find the unity that Jesus promises?

Just as importantly, how can we be *sure* of the truth? For we are only human, and our reach is limited. I can sit on my couch, reading the New Testament, but like the Ethiopian eunuch who encountered the apostle Philip on the road, I wonder, *who will explain this to me?* (see Acts 8:26-40).

And then this Jesus of whom we read in the gospels, whom we are meeting and getting to know through his words, used *more* than words when he was on earth. He did not just teach. He healed. He shared meals. He fed the hungry. He forgave sins and made broken lives whole. He didn't hover above the crowds and let his words drift down into people's spirits. He had a *body*. He moved, spoke, touched, forgave, healed, died, and rose with that *body*. Finally, at the very end, he gathered his apostles—such a disparate, flawed group of men!—and sent them out to the whole world to baptize in his name, assuring them that he would be with them always (Matthew 28:20).

He would be with them always. Not just his spirit, his ideas, his goals, or his intentions—but *he* would be with them always.

It's not unreasonable to wonder how.

Spiritual but Not Religious

It isn't surprising that many of us think of "church" in either negative, or at the very least, neutral terms.

Some of us have had very negative experiences of church. Perhaps we have been mistreated by a church authority or employee or simply found what we experienced as church to be spiritually limiting instead of freeing. As it was all presented to us, perhaps the whole church business seemed much more about control, power, buildings, and ritual for its own sake. We may have heard a lot of talk about maintaining and building an institution, but not much about venturing outside that institution and reaching the lost sheep with Jesus' love.

Even if we don't feel quite so negatively, we might not be willing to allow church to play a central role in our spirituality, either.

The idea that "I'm spiritual, but not religious" or "I don't really need church to be in a relationship with Jesus" isn't uncommon, even among Catholics. There's a sense that church might have its place—to maintain tradition for those who need it, to provide a sort of ritual that we know we need at least once in a while, to provide fellowship with other Christians or a nice place for weddings and funerals. But ultimately, many believe that it's really not that important. Jesus comes to me on my own. I make of him what I can, and church doesn't really help much in that journey, and might even hurt.

There are a number of sources for these feelings. Protestant Christians, especially evangelicals, are rooted in the centrality of the individual's relationship with God, one in which church functions as a place for fellowship and for Christians to corporately serve, but that is not any kind of organic necessity to the Christian life. Americans are famously individualistic—our entire political and economic system is built on individualism—so it is not surprising that we absorb this sensibility into our thinking about religion.

And finally, there is the difficult but simple truth that for whatever reason, many Catholics have not experienced the powerful, life-giving presence of Jesus Christ as they have worshipped, learned, listened, and simply lived their lives in the Catholic Church. It may be their own fault, or it may be the fault of preachers, catechists, and even families—but the fact is that when the second-largest Christian "denomination" in the United States is ex-Catholics, you know something is wrong.

Pope Benedict has noticed this phenomenon as well. Long ago, at the very beginning of his life as a priest, he served in a parish in the suburbs of Munich—a busy, active parish with all types of activities, including youth ministry, of which he was put in charge. He came out of the experience with deep concern—that the external, apparent health of the institution disguised a problem. As one commentator noted:

> In a climate that might have led to triumphalism, the young priest-professor Ratzinger had collected in 1958, in an article written for the magazine *Hochland*, the reflections suggested by the brief but intense pastoral experience gone through some years earlier as chaplain in the parish of the Precious Blood in Bogenhausen, the upper-class district of Munich. He described as a statistical "trick" the cliché that portrays Europe as "a continent almost wholly Christian." The Church in the post-war world seemed to him a "Church of pagans. No longer, as once, a Church of pagans become Christians, but a Church of pagans who still call themselves Christians and in truth have become pagans." He spoke of a new paganism "that grows without letting in the heart of the Church and threatens to demolish it from the inside."[44]

In other words, most of the people whom he was serving were not making a profound connection between their lives, Jesus, and the Church. He did not blame the individuals, but instead sensed that there was something missing in the Church's presentation of its ancient truths, and this gap would produce great trouble down the road. This intuition was what led Fr. Ratzinger to be such an enthusiastic supporter of the fundamental program of the Second Vatican Council, as well as part of what inspired him in his theological method.

As we read Ratzinger then and Pope Benedict now, we can pick up the fruit of these earlier observations of the disconnect that people experience between life and Church. It is not difficult to find:

> This friendship with Jesus is not a friendship with an unreal person, with someone who belongs to the past or who is distant from human beings, seated at God's right hand. Jesus is present in his body, which is still a body of flesh and blood: he is the Church, the communion of the Church.[45]

God loves us and this world enough to have created it all. He wants it—us—to exist. We have strayed, we turn from him, we refuse to return his love, we refuse to love the rest of his creation the way he does.

God wants to touch us, to bring us back; he wants us to live *in* him, to be freed from the sin and death that separates us from him, each other, and even our truest selves, which first began in Genesis. The sin of Adam and Eve separates them first from each other, as they dissemble and place blame; then from their true selves, as they feel shame and discomfort in their own bodies; and then from him, as they must leave the place God had created for them.

God puts all of this right in Jesus Christ, and not just for those who lived in Palestine two thousand years ago, but for us, here and now. That means that Jesus can reach us today, and we can reach back, that we can be taken up into Jesus' very life, which is the life of God.

Church is not an obligation, an extra in our Christian spiritual journey. To know Jesus in the most intimate, life-giving way, we know him through his body, the Church. It's a gift.

The Body of Christ on Earth

If you read both the gospels and St. Paul's letters, you see this organic understanding of church very clearly. Paul doesn't speak of the Church as a gathering of like-minded believers—he speaks of it, several times, as *the body of Christ* (1 Corinthians 12:12-31; Colossians 1:18; 2:18-20; Ephesians 1:22-23; 4:12).

And how does one become part of Christ's body on earth? Through baptism, Paul says, which is far more than a sign to which we show others that we believe or an essentially external ritual indicating membership. In baptism, we die and rise again. We become new creatures. Christ lives in us, and we in him. And together, we are the Church, and through this Church, Jesus is present in the world:

Thus, the Church, despite all the human frailties that mark her historical profile, is revealed as a marvelous creation of love, brought into being to bring Christ close to every man and every woman who truly desire to meet him, until the end of time. And in the Church, the Lord always remains our contemporary. Scripture is not something of the past. The Lord does not speak in the past but speaks in the present; he speaks to us today, he enlightens us, he shows us the way through life, he gives us communion, and thus he prepares us and opens us to peace.[46]

As he does so skillfully, here Pope Benedict takes a gospel passage and helps us see more deeply into the relationship of Jesus and his Church. He is discussing Jesus' healing of Peter's mother-in-law (Matthew 8:14-15):

Jesus' entire mission is symbolically portrayed in this episode. Jesus, coming from the Father, visited people's homes on our earth and found a humanity that was sick, sick with fever, the fever of ideologies, idolatry, forgetfulness of God. The Lord gives us his hand, lifts us up, and heals us.

And he does so in all ages; he takes us by the hand with his Word, thereby dispelling the fog of ideologies and forms of idolatry. He takes us by the hand in the sacraments; he heals us from the fever of our passions and sins through absolution in the Sacrament of Reconciliation. He gives us the possibility to raise ourselves, to stand before God and before men and women. And precisely with this content of the Sunday liturgy, the Lord comes to meet us, he takes us by the hand, raises us and heals us ever anew with the gift of his words, the gift of himself.[47]

And in another context, in a homily discussing a passage from the Book of Revelation, the pope alludes to the first chapter of John's Gospel, in which we read of the Word—the *Logos*, Jesus—dwelling among us, or "pitching his tent":

God is not far from us, he is not somewhere out in the universe, somewhere that none of us can go. He has pitched his tent among us: in Jesus he became one of us, flesh and blood just like us. This is his "tent." And in the ascension, he did not go somewhere far away from us. His tent, he himself in his body, remains among us and is one of us. We can call him by name and speak at ease with him. He listens to us and, if we are attentive, we can also hear him speaking back.

Let me repeat: in Jesus it is God who "camps" in our midst. But let me also repeat: where exactly does this happen? Our reading gives us two answers to this question. It says that the men and women at peace "have washed their robes and made them white in the blood of the Lamb" (Revelation 7:14). To us this sounds very strange. In his cryptic language, the seer is speaking about baptism. His words about "the blood of the Lamb" allude to Jesus' love, which he continued to show even up to his violent death. This love, both divine and human, is the bath into which he plunges us at baptism—the bath with which he washes us, cleansing us so that we can be fit for God and capable of living in his company.[48]

We have not been left alone. We have not even been left simply with a book and our wits. Jesus promised he would be with his disciples always. *And he is.*

From There to Here

Yet even if I believe that Jesus is present in his gathered, baptized disciples, what is the problem with thinking of that reality as simply a group with shared beliefs and a Bible? Is there more to it than that?

Yes, simply because that a group with shared beliefs and a Bible is, because it is human, going to find staying on track and staying faithful to be a difficult road. We only need to look at Christian history to see how true that is, to see the divisions and heresies that have emerged over time.

Jesus promised he would be with us until the end of time. Wouldn't he, out of love, surely leave us some way in which what he gave us on earth could be faithfully transmitted to us today, so that we would, in full confidence and certainty, know that the words we are hearing are Jesus' words and the actions we are experiencing are those of Christ who loves us so?

Pope Benedict addresses this question frequently, explaining the gift of assurance in Jesus' presence in the Church and where it comes from. In fact, he reminds us that there is no way to know Jesus *without* the Church. There is no magical connection between our hearts and minds and the first century. The only way we know Jesus is through the Church. It is because of the Church that we know Jesus, which is why it is his body:

> . . . A slogan that was popular some years back, "Jesus yes, Church no," is totally inconceivable with the intention of Christ. This individualistically chosen Jesus is an imaginary Jesus.
>
> We cannot have Jesus without the reality he created and in which he communicates himself. Between the Son of God-made-flesh and his Church, there is a profound, unbreakable, and mysterious continuity by which Christ is present today in his people. He is always contemporary with us, he is always contemporary with the Church, built on the

foundation of the apostles and alive in the succession of the apostles. And his very presence in the community, in which he himself is always with us, is the reason for our joy. Yes, Christ is with us, the kingdom of God is coming.[49]

The apostles weren't just accidental followers who happened to keep meeting and preaching about Jesus. Through them and their ministry, as it continues today, we know Jesus.

What the apostles represent in the relationship between the Lord Jesus and the Church of the origins is similarly represented by the ministerial succession in the relationship between the primitive Church and the Church of today. It is not merely a material sequence; rather, it is a historical instrument that the Spirit uses to make the Lord Jesus, head of his people, present through those who are ordained for the ministry through the imposition of hands and the bishops' prayer.

Consequently, through apostolic succession, it is Christ who reaches us: in the words of the apostles and of their successors, it is he who speaks to us; through their hands, it is he who acts in the sacraments; in their gaze it is his gaze that embraces us and makes us feel loved and welcomed into the heart of God. And still today, as at the outset, Christ himself is the true Shepherd and Guardian of our souls whom we follow with deep trust, gratitude, and joy.[50]

When we encounter Jesus today—through his word in the New Testament, through his teaching, through the sacraments, through the spiritual and corporal works of mercy—we encounter him, not because of a magical leap from yesterday to today, but because of the faithfulness of his disciples, preserving what he had taught and done, passing it on, and most importantly, embodying it in their own ministry so that we, today, might know Jesus.

Many Parts

Even if we understand this, another temptation often presents itself: to limit our thinking about Church to our own parish, in our own part of the world, in our own time.

But that is not what Church is, because in the Church, we meet Christ, who transcends the boundaries of space and time. In and through our life in the body of Christ, we are joined to God and to each other, the way God wants his creation to be united to him—in love.

In remembering the first World Youth Day of his papacy, in Cologne, Germany, Pope Benedict reflected on this reality:

In Cologne, the young people encountered and adored Emmanuel, God-with-us, in the mystery of the Eucharist, and they came to understand better that the Church is the great family through which God creates a space of communion and unity between every continent, culture, and race, a family vaster than the world that knows limits and boundaries; a "great band of pilgrims," so to speak, who walk together with Christ, guided by him, the bright star that illumines history.[51]

Speaking on Pentecost to representative of "New Movements"—groups dedicated to living out the gospel in various, diverse ways—Benedict pointed to the holy diversity in the body of Christ:

> But in him multiplicity and unity go hand in hand. He breathes where he wills. He does so unexpectedly, in unexpected places and in ways previously unheard of. And with what diversity and corporality does he do so! And it is precisely here that diversity and unity are inseparable.
>
> He wants your diversity, and he wants you for the one body, in union with the permanent orders—the joints—of the Church, with the successors of the apostles and with the successor of St. Peter.[52]

And of course, this unity extends across time as well:

> Dear friends, during Vespers this evening, we are united in thought and prayer with the voices of the countless men and women who have chanted this psalm in this very place [Notre Dame Cathedral, Paris] down the centuries. We are united with the pilgrims who went up to Jerusalem and to the steps of its Temple, and with the thousands of men and women who understood that their earthly pilgrimage was to end in heaven, in the eternal Jerusalem, trusting Christ to guide them there. What joy indeed, to know that we are invisibly surrounded by so great a crowd of witnesses![53]

Sometimes, though, there is a problem with how we think about unity. We think it is something that we bring about, that we create. Through our social events, through our ice-breaking and community-building techniques, through our efforts to make Mass "more meaningful," *we* bring unity to the body of Christ. But this is not so—as Paul says over and over, and as Pope Benedict reiterates here. It's Jesus who unifies us, whether we sense it or not. When we are baptized, when we share Eucharist, *we are unified in Christ:*

> Christ personally unites himself with each one of us, but Christ himself is also united with the man and the woman who are next to me. And the bread is for me but it is also for the other. Thus Christ unites all of us with himself and all of us with one another. In communion we receive Christ. But Christ is likewise united with my neighbor: Christ and my neighbor are inseparable in the Eucharist. And thus we are all one bread and one body. A Eucharist without solidarity with others is a Eucharist abused. And here we come to the root and, at the same time, the kernel of the doctrine on the Church as the body of Christ, of the Risen Christ.[54]

Here I meet Jesus Christ. It doesn't matter whether I can feel anything special or not. Sometimes I will, sometimes I won't. Similarly, in a marriage, it doesn't matter how I feel about my spouse at any particular moment—we are still bound by our vows, united as one in Christ. It doesn't matter how angry I get with my children or how distant they may feel from me—we are still who we are, parents and children.

I meet Jesus in his body, the Church. He feeds me, heals me, speaks to me, guides me, forgives me, saves me from death. And he meets every one of my brothers and sisters in him, in exactly the same way, and through him, boundaries are broken, and love—eternal love—shapes and forms us.

Do I know this? Are my eyes opened enough to meet Jesus in this way he so graciously comes to me? Am I ready, as Pope Benedict likes to say so often, for the adventure?

When the Body Hurts

As we've mentioned, many find it difficult to meet Jesus in the body of Christ because they experience it as corrupt and flawed. Pope Benedict, as a lifelong Catholic, a priest for almost sixty years, and the prefect of the congregation that was charged with handling some aspects of clerical sexual abuses cases, is fully aware of this reality and doesn't shy away from speaking of it.

Just weeks before being elected pope in 2005, Cardinal Ratzinger wrote the meditations for the Way of the Cross, which is prayed at the Colosseum every Good Friday. The Ninth Station—Jesus falling for the third time—gave him an opportunity for a searing, honest reflection on how the body of Christ, the Church, falls and suffers because of its members:

> What can the third fall of Jesus under the cross say to us? We have considered the fall of man in general, and the falling of many Christians away from Christ and into a godless secularism. Should we not also think of how much Christ suffers in his own Church? How often is the holy sacrament of his Presence abused, how often must he enter empty and evil hearts! How often do we celebrate only

ourselves, without even realizing that he is there! How often is his Word twisted and misused! What little faith is present behind so many theories, so many empty words! How much filth there is in the Church, and even among those who, in the priesthood, ought to belong entirely to him! How much pride, how much self-complacency! What little respect we pay to the Sacrament of Reconciliation, where he waits for us, ready to raise us up whenever we fall! All this is present in his passion. His betrayal by his disciples, their unworthy reception of his Body and Blood, is certainly the greatest suffering endured by the Redeemer; it pierces his heart. We can only call to him from the depths of our hearts: *Kyrie eleison*—Lord, save us.[55]

At St. Patrick's Cathedral in New York City in 2008, Pope Benedict called on those in the Church to bring others inside to see its beauty and glory:

This is no easy task in a world which can tend to look at the Church, like those stained glass windows, "from the outside": a world which deeply senses a need for spirituality, yet finds it difficult to "enter into" the mystery of the Church. Even for those of us within, the light of faith can be dimmed by routine, and the splendor of the Church obscured by the sins and weaknesses of her members.[56]

There is no doubt that Christ's body continues to be crucified, not only from those in the world who would persecute him, but also from within. Pope Benedict calls on us to frequently examine our lives and how we, as a Church, live out our mission, and to be open to reform, to change, and to repentance. On Palm Sunday in 2008, he asked:

Is our faith sufficiently pure and open so that starting from it, "pagans," the people today who are seeking and who have their questions, can intuit the light of the one God, associate themselves in the atriums of faith with our prayers and, with their questions, perhaps also become worshippers? Does the awareness that greed is idolatry enter our heart too and the praxis of our life? Do we not perhaps in various ways let idols enter even the world of our faith? Are we disposed to let ourselves be ceaselessly purified by the Lord, letting him expel from us and the Church all that is contrary to him?[57]

Practically speaking, this means we must stay close to Christ:

The parish, the living cell of the Church, must also really be a place of inspiration, life, and solidarity which helps people build together centers in the periphery. And I must say here, there is often talk about the Church in the suburbs and in the center, which would be Rome, but in fact in the Church there are no suburbs because where Christ is, the whole center is there.

Wherever the Eucharist is celebrated, wherever the Tabernacle stands, there is Christ; hence, there is the center, and we must do all we can to ensure that these living centers are effective, present, and truly a force that counters this marginalization.[58]

The mystery of the Church is not one that is explained away or disguised. Peter, the first pope, denied Jesus. The early Christian community had to deal with division, even on important theological matters, from the very beginning. Human beings fail. We fail, every day, in responding to Jesus' call—every one of us, not just the ordained—to give of ourselves in selfless love. That's another reason we don't depend on ourselves—we depend on Christ, and open ourselves so he can work through us.

Spread the Good News

So to meet Jesus, we come to him through his Church. God is everywhere, and God works in the hearts of every person, but in the Church we have received an astonishing gift from Christ himself—his own loving presence. I yearn for the eternal joy of life in God. I read the Scriptures and learn that it is real and true, and that my yearning has been answered in Jesus, who speaks to me with words I understand, who loves me with God's very own love. And in those same Scriptures, I find another promise—a promise not only that he is with *me*, but that he is with *us*, and *we* are his body. In this body I can be nourished, loved, and forgiven by *him*, and then go forth and spread this very, very Good News:

> May each one of you rediscover God as the sense and foundation of every creature, light of truth, flame of charity, bond of unity, like the hymn of the *Agorà* of the Italian youth. May you be docile to the power of the Spirit! He, the Holy Spirit . . . makes you witnesses of Christ. Not in

word but in deed, with a new type of life. You will not be afraid any longer to lose your freedom, because you will live it fully by giving it away in love. You will no longer be attached to material goods, because you will feel within you the joy of sharing them. You will cease to be sad with the sadness of the world, but you will feel sorrow at evil and rejoice at goodness, especially for mercy and forgiveness. And if this happens, if you will have truly discovered God in the face of Christ, you will no longer think of the Church as an institution external to you, but as your spiritual family, as we are living now, at this moment. This is the faith that your forefathers have handed down to you. This is the faith you are called to live today, in very different times.[59]

CHAPTER SIX

MEETING JESUS
IN THE LITURGY

*At the beginning of this Holy Mass, let us pray the Lord that
he may take from us all that is old, and that he may shatter
our former withdrawal into self as well as our self-sufficiency
in order to make us new.*[60]

Anyone who lives with or even works with teenagers is famil-
iar with these questions: "Why do I have to go to church?"
"Why did I have to be baptized?" "Do I have to be confirmed?"
"Why do I have to go to confession?"

It's not difficult to discern a common theme, summed up in the
words "have to": obligation, necessity, requirement.

Perhaps these questions have haunted us too, no matter what
our age. Barely awake on a Sunday morning, anticipating yet
another flat homily and uninspiring music, we wonder if we
have to go. Contemplating the diversity of human cultures and
religions, we wonder why anyone would have to be baptized.
Uncomfortable and ashamed, we wonder about this confession
business indeed.

Duty is associated with religion for good reasons, just as duty
is associated with any relationship for good reason. We love our
spouses and our children, but since emotion and passion can't
carry the day, all day, every day, we accept the duty to serve

and sacrifice beyond our own desires as a part of that love. So it is, built into religious practice, an understanding of the duty to actively worship, serve, and give thanksgiving to the loving God who made us, on whom we are totally dependent for life.

We are, indeed, commanded to honor, commanded to serve, commanded to worship. And commanded incidentally, by Jesus, to love.

But what is also true is that this sense of duty, which tends to be an important part of our faith formation as children, can sometimes stick with us as we grow into adults in unhealthy ways—ways that may even stunt us and impede us in our journey.

What was our baptism all about? Joining a group? A recognition of our birth, our physical existence? Getting a certificate that permits us to move on to other milestones?

What is the Mass, the Eucharist in our lives? A weekly gathering of friends and acquaintances? A time to affirm our Catholic identity, because that is what Catholics do? The one hour of our week during which we focus on God?

Why do we worship, participate in the sacraments, pray with others? Is it because this is just what Catholics do, and it joins us loosely to God, and we know this reality through the pleasantness of the experience or the emotion it engenders?

And does any of it, from baptism on, make any difference in how we live?

Real Presence

"Liturgy" refers to worship in general, and in Catholicism our liturgical life covers much ground, but in this chapter we'll focus on the sacraments, since that is the core, the spring from which everything else flows, particularly baptism and the Eucharist.

At this point, it won't be any surprise to learn that the liturgical life of Catholics is of great interest to Pope Benedict. His childhood faith was profoundly impacted by the Mass as well as by other devotions and liturgical practices. As a theologian, he has written extensively on the Eucharist in particular, and has been deeply concerned about the liturgical life of Catholics since the Second Vatican Council.

Those with only a superficial knowledge of Pope Benedict's writings and the dynamics of Catholic life since the early 1960s tend to caricature his thought on this matter, claiming that his priority is to "turn back the clock" on the liturgical reforms of the Second Vatican Council, and to do so for the sake of nostalgia, fear, or clericalism. This is simply untrue.

There is not the time or space here to fully delve into Pope Benedict's history on the matter of liturgy, so a brief account will have to do.

Two mistaken assumptions about the liturgical changes that occurred in the wake of the council often prevail: first, that these changes were all rather sudden and purely a result of the spirit of the 1960s; and second, that everything that indeed happened in most parishes was actually mandated by the council.

The "liturgical movement" had been a part of Catholic life since the nineteenth century, increasing in energy after World War II as scholars and pastoral ministers sought to find ways to help Catholics connect more deeply with Christ through the liturgy. Some of these efforts involved better catechesis and others involved examining how the liturgy itself might adapt, such as use of the vernacular. Joseph Ratzinger, while not directly involved in the liturgical movement, was certainly critical of some aspects of it—those that he felt were putting the priorities of scholars above the realities of how ordinary people lived and worshipped. However, he was still supportive of and nourished by much of the work of those who had as a priority to help individual Catholics deepen their liturgical lives.

In addition, much of what happened so quickly after the Second Vatican Council was not explicitly mandated by the council documents, which called, for example, for more use of the vernacular but not a total replacement of Latin by the vernacular; which never mentioned the stance of the priest during Mass; which never encouraged the diminishing of individual devotions.

Much of what Pope Benedict wrote about before his election—and his efforts regarding liturgy since then—have been in service of helping to retrieve what the Second Vatican Council really said and intended about liturgy. He has also tried to help Catholics today simply understand that Catholic liturgical life is a continuity—what was sacred yesterday cannot cease to be sacred today—and to help us become whole again, liturgically, by reattaching ourselves to the myriad and rich ways that the Spirit has worked through Catholic liturgical life in the past.

Even though these matters are not dealt with directly in this chapter, clearing up those misconceptions can help Catholics begin to listen to what Pope Benedict has to say about the liturgy. For what they will find, as they read what Pope Benedict has written about liturgy over the past few years, is in line with everything else he has said so far: through the sacraments, the devotions, the liturgical year—the entire liturgical life of the Church—Jesus meets us. He reaches out to us, embraces us, makes himself available and vulnerable to us, draws us into intimacy with him and with our brothers and sisters, and reconciles the world.

He is *present. Really present.*

Born Again

In the early Church, new believers were initiated only at the Easter Vigil—moving from the darkness of Jesus' death to the light of resurrection and eternal life. At his homilies at the Easter Vigils at St. Peter's Basilica, Pope Benedict has spoken powerfully of this reality to all of us, and especially to those whom he would be baptizing:

So, dear friends, it is clear that, through baptism, the mysterious words spoken by Jesus at the Last Supper become present for you once more. In baptism, the Lord enters your life through the door of your heart. We no longer stand alongside or in opposition to one another. He passes through all these doors. This is the reality of baptism: he, the risen One, comes; he comes to you and joins his life with yours, drawing you into the open fire of his love. You become one, one with him, and thus one among yourselves. At first this can sound rather abstract and unrealistic. But the more you live the life of the baptized, the more you can experience the truth of these words. Believers—the baptized—are never truly cut off from one another. Continents, cultures, social structures, or even historical distances may separate us. But when we meet, we know one another on the basis of the same Lord, the same faith, the same hope, the same love, which form us. . . . We are in communion because of our deepest identity: Christ within us. Thus faith is a force for peace and reconciliation in the world: distances between people are overcome; in the Lord we have become close (cf. Ephesians 2:13). . . .

This is exactly what happens in baptism: he draws us toward himself; he draws us into true life. He leads us through the often murky sea of history, where we are frequently in danger of sinking amid all the confusion and perils. In baptism he takes us, as it were, by the hand; he leads us along the path that passes through the Red Sea of this life and introduces us to everlasting life, the true and upright life. Let us grasp his hand firmly! Whatever may happen, whatever may befall us, let us not lose hold of his hand! Let us walk along the path that leads to life.[61]

One of the wonderful realities that Pope Benedict challenges us to remember—and live—is that being joined to Jesus in baptism is not just a single moment, and it is not even just a present moment. It is a moment encompassing eternity, in which we die and rise with Christ and therefore are joined to God's eternal, cosmic love. As he said to those gathered for the baptism of several infants in 2009:

If, with this sacrament, the newly baptized becomes an adoptive child of God, the object of God's infinite love that safeguards him and protects him from the dark forces of the evil one, it is necessary to teach the child to recognize

God as Father and to be able to relate to him with a filial attitude. And, therefore, when in accordance with the Christian tradition as we are doing today, children are baptized and introduced into the light of God and of his teachings, no violence is done to them. Rather, they are given the riches of divine life in which is rooted the true freedom that belongs to the children of God,a freedom that must be educated and modeled as the years pass to render it capable of responsible personal decisions.

Dear parents, dear godfathers and godmothers, I greet you all with affection and join in your joy for these little ones who today are reborn into eternal life. May you be aware of the gift received and never cease to thank the Lord who, with today's sacrament, introduces your children into a new family, larger and more stable, more open and more numerous than your own; I am referring to the family of believers, to the Church, to a family that has God as Father and in which all recognize one another as brothers and sisters in Jesus Christ.

Today, therefore, you are entrusting your children to God's goodness, which is a force of light and love, and they, even amid life's difficulties, will never feel abandoned if they stay united with him. Therefore, be concerned with educating them in the faith, teaching them to pray and grow as Jesus did and with his help, "in wisdom and in stature, and in favor with God and man" (cf. Luke 2:52).[62]

At the Easter Vigil in 2006, also an occasion for baptisms, Pope Benedict challenged our common thinking on baptism:

Baptism is something quite different from an act of ecclesial socialization, from a slightly old-fashioned and complicated rite for receiving people into the Church. It is also more than a simple washing, more than a kind of purification and beautification of the soul. It is truly death and resurrection, rebirth, transformation to a new life.

How can we understand this? I think that what happens in baptism can be more easily explained for us if we consider the final part of the short spiritual autobiography that St. Paul gave us in his Letter to the Galatians. Its concluding words contain the heart of this biography: "It is no longer I who live, but Christ who lives in me" (Galatians 2:20). I live, but I am no longer I. The "I," the essential identity of man—of this man, Paul—has been changed. He still exists, and he no longer exists. He has passed through a "not," and he now finds himself continually in this "not": I, but no longer I.[63]

So my challenge is clear: as Paul says, it is no longer I who live, but Christ who lives in me. This is humbling and awesome—in the fullest sense—but it is not magic either. Jesus comes to me, but like any gift, if that presence is to make a difference in my life, I must accept it. As Catholics used to speak of it (and some probably still do), it is about cooperating with the grace of God, which is essentially the presence of God in my life.

Not an obligation, necessarily, but a gift. What, after all, do I seek? I know that no matter what the particularities of my journey, I am searching for love and meaning and eternal life and joy. In baptism, as Pope Benedict says, Jesus takes my hand.

So many years after my own baptism, am I still holding on?

Hand in Hand with Jesus

Baptism is only the beginning of the journey, of course. Jesus remains with us, as we've seen, in his word; in the Church, his body; and the other sacraments, gifts of Jesus' presence—his own gifts. After baptism, the most intimate continuing encounters we have with Jesus are, of course, through the Eucharist.

Our First Communions were a big deal. But it's almost inevitable that in the years since then, our sense of Jesus' presence in the Eucharist has been dulled by familiarity and routine, and perhaps even by externally uninspiring liturgies as well as our own challenges of faith.

Listening to Pope Benedict, we are invited to dig more deeply, to abandon the paradigm of obligation and routine, and to welcome the full, Real Presence of Jesus in the Eucharist.

The Eucharist is mysterious and profound, but at its heart, it bears a simplicity that frames Pope Benedict's words about his own First Communion, shared with a group of children:

At the heart of my joyful and beautiful memories is this one: . . . I understood that Jesus had entered my heart, he had actually visited me. And with Jesus, God himself was with me. And I realized that this is a gift of love that is truly worth more than all the other things that life can give.

So on that day I was really filled with great joy, because Jesus came to me and I realized that a new stage in my life was beginning, I was nine years old, and that it was henceforth important to stay faithful to that encounter, to that communion. I promised the Lord as best I could: "I always want to stay with you," and I prayed to him, "but above all, stay with me." So I went on living my life like that; thanks be to God, the Lord has always taken me by the hand and guided me, even in difficult situations.[64]

Jesus taking us by the hand—Pope Benedict is fond of this image of Christ staying with us. As we have seen so often, Pope Benedict reminds us that God is *not* invisible. He comes to us in Jesus, remains with us in his Church, and lives among us in the Eucharist:

This is the deepest purpose of this sacred building's existence: the Church exists so that in it we may encounter Christ, Son of the living God. God has a Face. God has a Name. In Christ, God was made flesh and gave himself to us in the mystery of the Most Holy Eucharist.

The Word is flesh. It is given to us under the appearances of bread and thus truly becomes the Bread on which we live. We live on Truth. This Truth is a Person: he speaks to us and we speak to him. The Church is the place of our encounter with the Son of the living God and thus becomes the place for the encounter among ourselves. This is the joy that God gives us: that he made himself one of us, that we can touch him, and that he dwells among us. The joy of God is our strength.[65]

Listening to Pope Benedict, the questions we ask rapidly shift. It is no longer, "Do I have to go?" but "How can I stay away?"

Communion

We have to be careful, though, don't we? The temptation to individualism in our religious faith is great. We forget that the God who loves us so much loves every other person in the world just as much as he loves us—no more, but no less either. We forget that we don't say "My Father" when we pray but "Our Father." We forget that Jesus' *commandment* was not only about loving God but loving each other.

Approaching Jesus in the Eucharist with open hearts, minds, and spirits, aware of who it is who meets us there, we are drawn into the reality that this is not just about me and Jesus. This is about me and Jesus and the rest of humanity and even the rest of the universe. I meet Jesus in the Eucharist, and in that meeting, I meet my brothers and sisters. It is truly *communion*. Through the sacrifice of Jesus, we are redeemed:

> In their hearts, people always and everywhere have somehow expected a change, a transformation of the world. Here now is the central act of transformation that alone can truly renew the world: violence is transformed into love, and death into life.
>
> Since this act transmutes death into love, death as such is already conquered from within, the resurrection is already present in it. Death is, so to speak, mortally wounded, so that it can no longer have the last word.
>
> To use an image well known to us today, this is like inducing nuclear fission in the very heart of being—the victory of love over hatred, the victory of love over death. Only this

intimate explosion of good conquering evil can then trigger off the series of transformations that little by little will change the world.[66]

One of the pope's traditional liturgical roles has been to lead a Eucharistic procession on the Feast of Corpus Christi, a procession that begins at St. John Lateran, the pope's cathedral in his role as bishop of Rome, up a hill to St. Maria Maggiore, another ancient basilica. In the homilies on these occasions over the past few years, the pope has spoken most eloquently on the role of the Eucharist, pulling together all of the themes we have encountered so far—our individual union with Jesus in the Eucharist, the communion between us that Jesus brings, and the reality of this Presence of Jesus, not just in the privacy of our hearts, not even within the walls of our church buildings, but into the entire world:

In the procession, we follow this sign, and in this way we follow Christ himself. And we ask of him: Guide us on the paths of our history! Show the Church and her pastors again and again the right path! Look at suffering humanity, cautiously seeking a way through so much doubt; look upon the physical and mental hunger that torments it! Give men and women bread for body and soul! Give them work! Give them light! Give them yourself! Purify and sanctify all of us! Make us understand that only through participation in your passion, through "yes" to the cross, to self-denial, to the purifications that you impose upon us, our lives can mature and arrive at true fulfillment. Gather us together from all corners of the earth. Unite your Church, unite wounded humanity! Give us your salvation! Amen.[67]

If the close relationship between the Last Supper and the mystery of Jesus' death on the cross is emphasized on Holy Thursday, [then] today, on the Feast of Corpus Christi, with the procession and unanimous adoration of the Eucharist, attention is called to the fact that Christ sacrificed himself for all humanity. His passing among the houses and along the streets of our city will be for those who live there an offering of joy, eternal life, peace, and love.

In the meantime, let us listen to his voice repeat, as we read in the Book of Revelation: "Behold, I stand at the door and knock; if any one hears my voice and opens the door, I will come in to him and eat with him, and he with me" (3:20).

The Feast of Corpus Christi wants to make the Lord's knocking audible, despite the hardness of our interior hearing. Jesus knocks at the door of our heart and asks to enter not only for the space of a day but forever.[68]

The Eucharist is a public devotion that has nothing esoteric or exclusive about it. Here too, this evening, we did not choose to meet one another; we came and find ourselves next to one another, brought together by faith and called to become one body, sharing the one Bread which is Christ. We are united over and above our differences of nationality, profession, social class, political ideas: we open ourselves to one another to become one in him. This has been a characteristic of Christianity from the outset, visibly fulfilled around the Eucharist, and it is always necessary to be alert to ensure that the recurring temptations of particularism, even if with good intentions, do not go in the opposite direction. Therefore Corpus Christi reminds us first of all of this: that being Christian means coming together from all parts of the world to be in the presence of the one Lord and to become one with him and in him.[69]

So in Jesus, we are met and embraced. We encounter the loving, suffering Jesus, risen again. He dwells within us, he binds us, and he nourishes us.

But why? Simply so we can feel refreshed and good about life, now and forever?

No, there is more here, as there always is. Jesus' presence on earth is not just about me and my feelings of security or fulfillment. In fact, it really isn't about that at all. It is about the redemption of the whole world, about being present in his body in order to redeem the world.

We are invited by Jesus to meet him and welcome his presence within us. But we are never nourished by anything simply so we can sit still. We are nourished so we can get up and get out into the world, strengthened and invigorated. With the Eucharist as our food, Jesus' very self as our food and drink, we move out into that world in, with, and for him—and the beloved children who still hunger. These words by Pope Benedict, addressed to a group of altar servers in 2006, are really for all of us:

The Eucharist is the source and summit of the bond of friendship with Jesus. You are very close to Jesus in the Eucharist, and this is the most important sign of his friendship for each one of us. Do not forget it.

This is why I am asking you not to take this gift for granted so that it does not become a sort of habit, knowing how it works and doing it automatically; rather, discover every day anew that something important happens, that the living God is among us, and that you can be close to him and help him so that his mystery is celebrated and reaches people.

If you do not give in to habit, if you put your innermost self into carrying out your service, then you will truly be his apostles and bear fruits of goodness and service in every context of your life: in the family, at school, in your free time.

Take to one and all that love which you receive in the liturgy, especially to places where you realize that they lack love, where they do not receive goodness, where they suffer and are lonely.

With the power of the Holy Spirit, try to take Jesus to those very people who are outcast, who are not very popular or have problems. With the power of the Holy Spirit, it is precisely there that you must take Jesus.

In this way, the Bread you see broken upon the altar will be shared and multiplied even more, and you, like the twelve apostles, will help Jesus distribute it to the people of today in their different walks of life.[70]

CHAPTER SEVEN

MEETING JESUS IN THE LITURGICAL YEAR

Advent means commemorating the first coming of the Lord in the flesh, with his definitive return already in mind, and, at the same time, it means recognizing that Christ present in our midst makes himself our traveling companion in the life of the Church who celebrates his mystery.[71]

O bjects: Three purple candles and one rose. Vestments of gold, green, white, or red. Somber-looking, violet-draped statues. Incense wafting upward. Smudges on foreheads. A single white candle, its flame silently witnessing to the Alpha and the Omega, the beginning and the end, flickering in expectant darkness on a cool spring night.

Sounds: Carols. Solitary chants recalling light and darkness, a happy fault and life breaking through. Silence. An alleluia resurrected after weeks of absence, the *Gloria* resounding again. Kneelers banging up and down, feet shuffling slowly, following the path trod in a city far away thousands of years ago.

People: Voices in the wilderness. Crowds rapturous, hungry, angry, then gone. Rulers, fishermen, cousins, shepherds. A mother.

Throughout the year they come and go, year after year, dependable, with only the slightest variation. The world turns on all kinds of years and seasons: nature, school, sports, fiscal. We rest, we bustle about, and then we rest again, but through all of them flows the liturgical year, with those familiar sights, sounds, and stories. Perhaps they are too familiar.

I once knew a priest who fell into a preaching pattern that became, after several years of hearing it, quite predictable. At the beginning of every Advent or Lent, year after year, he would begin his homily with a sigh and the phrase, "Here we go again," which seemed to assume that his congregation was weary and bored with the whole routine and needed a jolt.

Although some in his congregation might have shared those feelings, I am not sure it was wise to assume so, for the liturgical seasons are one of those aspects of the Christian life that we do seem to "get" and even more, maintain an interest in. There are times when we feel the pressing demands of these seasons— Christmas preparations, for example, or planning for spring break or Easter travel. But most people I know are grateful for this rhythm, glad to be guided along Jesus' journey, knowing that each time there is something new, because even though God stays the same, we don't.

Pope Benedict, preaching during all of these seasons of the year, has much to say to help us shake loose of any feelings of routine. He wants us to pay attention, because Jesus can speak to us through the ebb and flow of the liturgical year when we open our hearts to meet him there.

Emmanuel

The liturgical year begins with the First Sunday of Advent. Several weeks beforehand, as Ordinary Time draws to a close, the Scriptures turn with increasing urgency to the judgment and hope that await us at the end of our lives, at the end of time.

Advent finally begins, and with it, the prophets Isaiah and John the Baptist call us to confront our sins. But they also speak of peace, reconciliation, a banquet on God's mountain for all peoples, and the coming of the One who will bring this about.

> The Advent cry of hope then expresses, from the outset and very powerfully, the full gravity of our state, of our extreme need of salvation. It is as if to say: we await the Lord not in the same way as a beautiful decoration upon a world already saved, but as the only way of liberation from a mortal danger, and we know that he himself, the Liberator, had to suffer and die to bring us out of this prison.[72]

> We have said that this coming was unique: "the" coming of the Lord. Yet, there is not only the final coming at the end of time: in a certain sense the Lord always wants to come through us. And he knocks at the door of our hearts: are you willing to give me your flesh, your time, your life? This is the voice of the Lord, who also wants to enter our epoch; he wants to enter human life through us. He also seeks a living dwelling place in our personal lives. This is the coming of the Lord. Let us once again learn this in the season of Advent: the Lord can also come among us.[73]

Pope Benedict has written of God's answer to our hope—his incarnation—often and with great tenderness. We might think there is nothing more to say on the subject—even our own secular culture cannot erase the fact that this season is about the coming of the Christ Child, But then again, I wonder how deep our awareness of Jesus' incarnation actually is. To test yourself, try this: find a baby. You don't have to hold him; simply look at that baby wherever you find him—in the grocery store, in a stroller in the park, gazing at you from a mother's shoulder, staring at you in the Communion line. Now think: *This* is how God came to us, not as a magical or plastic sort of baby, but *this* sort of baby:

God's sign is simplicity. God's sign is the baby. God's sign is that he makes himself small for us. This is how he reigns. He does not come with power and outward splendor. He comes as a baby—defenseless and in need of our help. He does not want to overwhelm us with his strength. He takes away our fear of his greatness. He asks for our love, so he makes himself a child. He wants nothing other from us than our love, through which we spontaneously learn to enter into his feelings, his thoughts, and his will—we learn to live with him and to practice with him that humility of renunciation that belongs to the very essence of love. God made himself small so that we could understand him, welcome him, and love him.[74]

So every Advent, year after year, we are invited to admit our need for God and to find that need fulfilled as we embrace him, welcome him—meet him at Christmas—in the infant Jesus.

The Christmas season ends on the Feast of the Baptism of the Lord, and it is traditional on that day for the pope to baptize a number of babies in the Sistine Chapel. In 2008, the pope's homily elucidated the ways in which we meet Jesus during this season, and indeed, during the entire liturgical year:

> The cycle of the Christmas solemnities leads us to meditate on the birth of Jesus, announced by the angels who were surrounded with the luminous splendor of God; the Christmas season speaks to us of the star that guided the Magi of the East to the house in Bethlehem, and invites us to look to heaven, which opens above the Jordan as God's voice resounds. These are all signs through which the Lord never tires of repeating: "Yes, I am here. I know you. I love you. There is a path that leads from me to you. And there is a path that rises from you to me." The Creator assumed the dimensions of a child in Jesus, of a human being like us, to make himself visible and tangible. At the same time, by making himself small, God caused the light of his greatness to shine. For precisely by lowering himself to the point of defenseless vulnerability of love, he shows what his true greatness is indeed, what it means to be God.
>
> Christmas, and more generally the liturgical year, is exactly that drawing near to these divine signs, to recognize them as impressed into daily events, so that our hearts may be open to God's love. And if Christmas and Epiphany serve primarily to render us capable of seeing, of opening our eyes and hearts to the mystery of a God who comes to be with us, then we can say that the Feast of the Baptism of Jesus introduces us into the daily regularity of a personal relationship with him.[75]

In the Desert

We proclaim and meditate on Jesus' life and ministry—his teaching, parables, miracles, and interactions with the men and women of his time, as well as his call to the apostles—during Ordinary Time, those weeks and months between Advent and Lent and Easter and Advent. In the first segment of Ordinary Time, we meet Jesus calling his disciples and beginning his ministry, and we contemplate our response to that very same call directed at us. Then we enter into Lent, the weeks in which we immerse ourselves in the fullness of Jesus' radical, sacrificial love.

"Immerse" is an appropriate word, for it calls to mind our baptisms in which that relationship began, as well as the depth of it. We are not just being taught by him or trying to be more like him. We are stripping away all that keeps us from him, deepening the intimacy begun with our baptisms. We live with him, he lives in us, and when we journey with him during Lent, we journey into the heart of the passion, in which we, with him, die and rise.

Lent began as a preparation period for catechumens, as Pope Benedict explained at a General Audience in 2007:

From the outset, . . . Lent was lived as the season of immediate preparation for baptism, to be solemnly administered during the Easter Vigil. The whole of Lent was a journey toward this important encounter with Christ, this immersion in Christ, this renewal of life. We have already been baptized, but baptism is often not very effective in our daily life.

Therefore Lent is a renewed "catechumenate" for us too, in which once again we approach our baptism to rediscover and relive it in depth, to return to being truly Christian.

Lent is thus an opportunity to "become" Christian "anew," through a constant process of inner change and progress in the knowledge and love of Christ. Conversion is never once and for all but is a process, an interior journey through the whole of life.[76]

During Lent we fast, we pray more, and we pour ourselves out in sacrificial love for others. For what end? So I'll be healthier and weigh less at the end? So I'll feel more virtuous? So I'll feel more Catholic? No, there is more to it than that, as Pope Benedict explained on the first day of Lent in 2008:

Today, Ash Wednesday, we are taking up our Lenten journey, as we do every year, motivated by a more intense spirit of prayer and reflection, penance and fasting. We are entering a "strong" liturgical season which . . . invites us, indeed we might say challenges us, to impress a more decisive impetus upon our Christian existence. The reason is that our commitments, anxieties, and preoccupations cause us to relapse into habit, exposing us to the risk of forgetting what an extraordinary adventure Jesus has involved us in. We need to begin our demanding journey of evangelical life every day anew, reentering ourselves by pausing for restorative thought. With the ancient rite of the imposition of ashes, the Church ushers us into Lent as if into a long spiritual retreat that lasts for forty days.[77]

So often our lives are marked by activity and motives that have nothing to do with relationships and everything to do with our own desires for success, affirmation, or material goods. Then we have to ask ourselves: how intimate can I really be with others in that context? We have to stop, divest our lives of the unnecessary, the self-aggrandizing, and even the harmful in order to enrich our relationships with spouse, family members, or friends. Lent serves the same purpose in our relationship with God. Our lives are cluttered and our hearts are closed. We pray, fast, and give with the rest of the Church in order to meet Jesus again—to let him in.

He Is Risen

Holy Week and Easter are truly the center of the Christian's year, for during that time we walk with Jesus—since we are united to him through our baptisms—on his journey of sacrificial love. We are taken up in that journey, absorbed in it, and it becomes ours.

Pope Benedict's words on the days of this week point us to the intimacy available to us during this time—moments in which we are actually lifted out of time and space and joined to Jesus. As Pope Benedict speaks of these days, he always asks us to recognize that this is not the past we celebrate: it is our present reality, to live in the passion and resurrection of Jesus:

In the Palm Sunday procession we join with the crowd of disciples who in festive joy accompany the Lord during his entry into Jerusalem. Like them, we praise the Lord with a loud voice for all the miracles we have seen. Yes, we too have seen and still see today the wonders of Christ: how he brings men and women to renounce the comforts of their lives and devote themselves totally to the service of the suffering; how he gives men and women the courage to oppose violence and deceit, to make room for truth in the world; how, in secret, he persuades men and women to do good to others, to bring about reconciliation where there had been hatred, and to create peace where enmity had reigned.[78]

On Holy Thursday we join Jesus and the apostles in the upper room, deep in the mystery of Jesus' sharing of his own self in the washing of the feet and the bread and wine, anticipating the sacrifice to come:

God descends and becomes a slave; he washes our feet so that we may come to his table. In this, the entire mystery of Jesus Christ is expressed. In this, what redemption means becomes visible.

The basin in which he washes us is his love, ready to face death. Only love has that purifying power which washes the grime from us and elevates us to God's heights.

The basin that purifies us is God himself, who gives himself to us without reserve—to the very depths of his suffering and his death. He is ceaselessly this love that cleanses us; in the sacraments of purification—baptism and the Sacrament of Penance—he is continually on his knees at our feet and carries out for us the service of a slave, the service of purification, making us capable of God.

His love is inexhaustible, it truly goes to the very end.

"You are clean, but not all of you," the Lord says (John 13:10). This sentence reveals the great gift of purification that he offers to us, because he wants to be at table together with us, to become our food. "But not all of you"—the obscure mystery of rejection exists, which becomes apparent with Judas' act, and precisely on Holy Thursday, the day on which Jesus made the gift of himself, it should give us food for thought. The Lord's love knows no bounds, but man can put a limit on it.[79]

On Good Friday, the journey continues and intensifies, and only a few remain. Where are we on that afternoon, and where are we as the night descends?

Through the sorrowful Way of the Cross, the men and women of all ages, reconciled and redeemed by Christ's blood, have become friends of God, sons and daughters of the heavenly Father. "Friend" is what Jesus calls Judas, and he offers him the last and dramatic call to conversion. He calls each of us friend because he is the true friend of everyone. Unfortunately, we do not always manage to perceive the depth of this limitless love that God has for his creatures. For him there is no distinction of race or culture. Jesus Christ died to liberate the whole of humanity from ignorance of God, from the circle of hate and vengeance, from the slavery to sin. The cross makes us brothers and sisters.

Let us ask ourselves: but what have we done with this gift? What have we done with the revelation of the face of

God in Christ, with the revelation of God's love that conquers hate? Many, in our age as well, do not know God and cannot find him in the crucified Christ. Many are in search of a love or a liberty that excludes God. Many believe they have no need of God.

Dear friends: after having lived together Jesus' passion, let us this evening allow his sacrifice on the cross to question us. Let us permit him to put our human certainties in crisis. Let us open our hearts to him. Jesus is the truth that makes us free to love. Let us not be afraid: upon dying, the Lord saved sinners, that is, all of us. The apostle Peter wrote: Jesus "himself bore our sins in his body upon the cross, that we might die to sin and live to righteousness. By his wounds you have been healed" (1 Peter 2:24). This is the truth of Good Friday: on the cross, the Redeemer has restored to us the dignity that belongs to us, has made us adoptive sons and daughters of God whom he has created in his image and likeness.

Let us remain, then, in adoration before the cross. O Christ, crucified King, give us true knowledge of you, the joy for which we yearn, the love that fills our heart, thirsty for the infinite. This is our prayer for this evening, Jesus, Son of God, who died for us on the cross and was raised up on the third day.[80]

And finally, on Easter, beginning the night before as we wait in darkness, the reason for Jesus' suffering and death becomes clear, and we not only learn the truth, we share in it, we are a part of it. We live in the reality that we are no longer alone, and that, as Paul says, sin and death have no more power over us. Jesus reigns:

> The great explosion of the resurrection has seized us in baptism so as to draw us on. Thus we are associated with a new dimension of life into which, amid the tribulations of our day, we are already in some way introduced. To live one's own life as a continual entry into this open space: this is the meaning of being baptized, of being Christian. This is the joy of the Easter Vigil. The resurrection is not a thing of the past; the resurrection has reached us and seized us. We grasp hold of it, we grasp hold of the risen Lord, and we know that he holds us firmly even when our hands grow weak. We grasp hold of his hand, and thus we also hold on to one another's hands, and we become one single subject, not just one thing. I, but no longer I: this is the formula of Christian life rooted in baptism, the formula of the resurrection within time. I, but no longer I: if we live in this way, we transform the world. It is a formula contrary to all ideologies of violence; it is a program opposed to corruption and to the desire for power and possession.

"I live and you will live also," says Jesus in St. John's Gospel (14:19) to his disciples—that is, to us. We will live through our existential communion with him, through being taken up into him who is life itself. Eternal life, blessed immortality, we have not by ourselves or in ourselves, but through a relation—through existential communion with him who is Truth and Love and is therefore eternal: God himself. Simple indestructibility of the soul by itself could not give meaning to eternal life; it could not make it a true life. Life comes to us from being loved by him who is Life; it comes to us from living-with and loving-with him. I, but no longer I: this is the way of the cross, the way that "crosses over" a life simply closed in on the I, thereby opening up the road toward true and lasting joy.[81]

And we move on with Jesus through the Easter season, to Pentecost, to more Ordinary Time, as we complete another liturgical year and begin a new one with Advent once again.

But there is nothing dull about this cycle, just as there is really nothing dull about any relationship, fully and deeply lived—how can a relationship with God be dull! Our lives change and shift every day, our horizons widen and narrow, our concerns ebb and flow. In the liturgical year, we have the gift—and it is a gift—to let Jesus touch us in all the seasons of our lives through the seasons of his own.

Throughout the liturgical year, particularly in Holy Week and Easter Week, the Lord walks beside us and explains the Scriptures to us, makes us understand this mystery: everything speaks of him. And this should also make our hearts burn within us, so that our eyes too may be opened. The Lord is with us; he shows us the true path. Just as the two disciples recognized Jesus in the breaking of the bread, so today, in the breaking of the bread, let us too recognize his presence. The disciples of Emmaus recognized him and remembered the times when Jesus had broken the bread. And this breaking of the bread reminds us of the first Eucharist celebrated in the context of the Last Supper, when Jesus broke the bread and thus anticipated his death and resurrection by giving himself to the disciples. Jesus also breaks bread with us and for us, he makes himself present with us in the Holy Eucharist, he gives us himself and opens our hearts. In the Holy Eucharist, in the encounter with his Word, we too can meet and know Jesus at this two-fold table of the Word and of the consecrated bread and wine. Every Sunday the community thus relives the Lord's Passover and receives from the Savior his testament of love and brotherly service.

Dear brothers and sisters, may the joy of these days strengthen our faithful attachment to the Crucified and Risen Christ. Above all, may we let ourselves be won over by the fascination of his resurrection. May Mary help us to be messengers of the light and joy of Easter for all our brethren. Once again, I wish you all a Happy Easter.[82]

Chapter Eight

Meeting Jesus in Prayer

Each one of us can be on intimate terms with him; each can call upon him. The Lord is always within hearing. We can inwardly draw away from him. We can live turning our backs on him. But he always waits for us and is always close to us.[83]

Prayer is such a fundamental part of the Christian life. For most of us, prayer began at a young age, when we were taught to "say our prayers." As we go through life, however, our prayer changes.

For example, when I was a teenager, I got the impression that the only legitimate prayer was contemplation and meditation. "Rote" prayer, including the Rosary, was for children and the spiritually immature. I am not sure why I thought that I was better than such spiritual masters as Teresa of Ávila and Francis de Sales, who recognized the importance of different forms of prayer, including vocal, memorized prayer.

Eventually in my thirties, I learned that the world within my own head, uninformed by the words and gestures borne of thousands of years of Jewish and Christian prayer, was a very small place. I wanted to be in a bigger place, a place in which I did not pray alone but with God's people, drawn into Christ, together. I have monks to thank for the beginning of that learning process, monks who gathered in dark, cool chapels at the end of the day, chanting ancient psalms that spoke of praise and anger, joy and sorrow.

We hope that as we age, our prayer matures, survives dry spells, and flourishes. And yet, even as we grow in prayer, we still face challenges. I can pray any way and every way—with words, without, in song, deep in Scripture or the words of the saints—but obstacles can still remain, part of my own making, part of the world's.

Perhaps I have not quite outgrown my childhood understanding of prayer, and still see it in utilitarian terms, not as the foundation of my life. I have not grasped what Paul meant when he said, "Pray without ceasing" (1 Thessalonians 5:17), much less allowed myself to live that way.

Perhaps I am not as open to God as I think I am. Am I ready for *anything* God has to say to me? Or am I operating out of the assumption that I pray in order to have *my* plans affirmed by God?

Perhaps I have missed the point of prayer. I approach prayer because I want to feel better about myself or my life, or because I want some sort of magic to happen, or because I believe that prayer is anything I want it to be, whatever I feel like at the moment.

Perhaps I suspect that there is no point to prayer anyway, that God is too big and the gap between us impossibly great.

If these suspicions haunt us, if these obstacles stand in our way, they keep us from the heart of prayer—from meeting Jesus as he waits for us.

Across the Divide

As should be very clear by now, Pope Benedict speaks as often as he can about Jesus' invitation to all of us to be in relationship with him. The foundation of our response to this invitation is in prayer:

Love for Christ expresses itself in the will to harmonize our own life with the thoughts and sentiments of his heart. This is achieved through interior union based on the grace of the sacraments, strengthened by continuous prayer, praise, thanksgiving, and penance. We have to listen attentively to the inspirations that he evokes through his Word, through the people we meet, through the situations of daily life. To love him is to remain in dialogue with him, in order to know his will and to put it into effect promptly.[84]

So right away, we might experience a slight adjustment in our understanding of prayer. It is not about finding a comfortable inner space. It is about being in dialogue with Jesus.

It's worthwhile—and maybe a little scary—to consider who is at the forefront of our prayer. When we come to prayer, who is on our minds? Is it God, or is it ourselves?

The disciples asked Jesus to teach them how to pray. He responded with a prayer, which begins, not with an explanation of who we are and why we are there and what our troubles are, but with a hallowing of God: Our Father.

The question, then, is this: If I seek to meet Jesus in my prayer, is he at the center of my prayer, or am I? Am I really ready to listen? How open am I?

It seems to me that this gesture of openness is also the first gesture of prayer: being open to the Lord's presence and to his gift. This is also the first step in receiving something that we do not have, that we cannot have with the intention of acquiring it all on our own.

We must make this gesture of openness, of prayer—give me faith, Lord!—with our whole being. We must enter into this willingness to accept the gift and let ourselves, our thoughts, our affections, and our will be completely immersed in this gift.[85]

Openness involves at least two aspects: a commitment and will to accept whatever it is God sends or tells me, and a sensitivity to the presence of God in a busy world, in the midst of a busy life:

Thus, it is also an invitation to be sensitive to this presence of the Lord who is knocking at my door. We must not be deaf to him, because the ears of our heart are so full of the din of the world that we cannot hear this silent presence that is knocking at our door.

Let us at the same time consider whether we really are prepared to open the doors of our heart; or perhaps this heart is crammed with so many other things that there is no room in it for the Lord, and for the time being, we have no time for him. Thus, insensitive, dead to his presence, distracted by other things, we fail to hear the essential: the Lord, knocking at the door. He is close to us; hence, true joy, which is more powerful than all the sorrows of the world or of our lives, is at hand.[86]

Putting Jesus at the center, becoming aware of what distracts us from his presence, we can now focus on the purpose of prayer, which is deeply related to everything else Benedict has been saying to us so far: to be a Christian is to be "in Christ." It means to let Christ live in me and love through me.

The purpose of prayer is to help this happen. As I pray, I let Jesus in, and, most importantly, I allow everything about my life to be shaped by that presence. I am surrounded by many voices, both internally and externally, which want to lead me, and some of those I dearly would like to follow. But my faith in Jesus tells me that he is the one Voice that loves me, the only one worthy of trusting with my life.

So how can I recognize that voice unless I take time to listen, know, and be familiar with it? In speaking to Swiss bishops in 2006, the pope explored this question (which, incidentally, should tell us something—that the pope is under no illusion that bishops are beyond the need for education on this score). No matter who we are, there is always a call to go deeper in our relationship with Christ:

Learn to think as Christ thought, learn to think with him! And this thinking is not only the thinking of the mind, but also a thinking of the heart.

We learn Jesus Christ's sentiments when we learn to think with him and thus, when we learn to think also of his failure, of his passage through failure and of the growth of his love in failure.

If we enter into these sentiments of his, if we begin to practice thinking like him and with him, then joy for God is awakened within us, confident that he is the strongest; yes, we can say that love for him is reawakened within us. We feel how beautiful it is that he is there and that we can know him—that we know him in the face of Jesus Christ who suffered for us. I think this is the first thing: that we ourselves enter into vital contact with God—with the Lord Jesus, the living God. . . ."[87]

This personal openness to the Lord is one part of the picture. The other part is context. How do I know if what I am sensing in my prayer is the Lord's voice or that of my own desires? Does prayer actually work on those desires and reshape them?

Pope Benedict, reflecting on St. Augustine in his encyclical *Spe Salvi,* points us to an important dimension of prayer: praying shapes our prayer. St. Paul says, "We do not know how to pray as we ought" (Romans 8:26), meaning not that we don't know the words, but that we do not really know what we should be praying *for*. Our own needs and desires blind us to what God wants of us. One of the foundational ways to discern and grow more sensitive to the authentic voice of God in our prayer, is to always pray in the context of the Church: with the Scriptures, with the liturgical prayer of the Church, with the Spirit-formed tradition of the Church in mind. If we really want to meet Jesus in prayer, we don't come at it as a lone ranger. We trust that Jesus lives within his Church, and by knowing Jesus in the Church, we can more easily recognize his voice in the context of our own prayer:

To pray is not to step outside history and withdraw to our own private corner of happiness. When we pray properly, we undergo a process of inner purification which opens us up to God and thus to our fellow human beings as well. In prayer we must learn what we can truly ask of God—what is worthy of God. We must learn that we cannot pray against others. We must learn that we cannot ask for the superficial and comfortable things that we desire at this moment—that meager, misplaced hope that leads us away from God. We must learn to purify our desires and our hopes. We must free ourselves from the hidden lies with which we deceive ourselves. God sees through them, and when we come before God, we too are forced to recognize them. "But who can discern his errors? Clear me from hidden faults," prays the psalmist (Psalm 19:12). Failure to recognize my guilt, the illusion of my innocence, does not justify me and does not save me, because I am culpable for the numbness of my conscience and my incapacity to recognize the evil in me for what it is. If God does not exist, perhaps I have to seek refuge in these lies, because there is no one who can forgive me, no one who is the true criterion. Yet my encounter with God awakens my conscience in such a way that it no longer aims at self-justification, and is no longer a mere reflection of me and those of my contemporaries who shape my thinking, but it becomes a capacity for listening to the Good itself.

For prayer to develop this power of purification, it must on the one hand be something very personal, an encounter between my intimate self and God, the living God. On the other hand, it must be constantly guided and enlightened by the great prayers of the Church and of the saints, by liturgical prayer, in which the Lord teaches us again and again how to pray properly. Cardinal Nguyen Van Thuan, in his book of spiritual exercises, tells us that during his life there were long periods when he was unable to pray and that he would hold fast to the texts of the Church's prayer: the Our Father, the Hail Mary, and the prayers of the liturgy. Praying must always involve this intermingling of public and personal prayer. This is how we can speak to God and how God speaks to us. In this way, we undergo those purifications by which we become open to God and are prepared for the service of our fellow human beings. We become capable of the great hope, and thus we become ministers of hope for others. Hope in a Christian sense is always hope for others as well. It is an active hope, in which we struggle to prevent things moving toward the "perverse end." It is an active hope also in the sense that we keep the world open to God. Only in this way does it continue to be a truly human hope.[88]

Teach Us to Pray

Even with that central purpose—knowing and being one with the mind and heart of Christ—there are still as many ways to pray as there are human beings on the journey.

During his pontificate, Pope Benedict has taken special care to remind us of these many different ways, paying special attention to what some might call more traditional modes of prayer and devotion. Some of us might not know about these forms or be closed to them because of their associations with the past. We might be under the impression, as I once was, that the only "real" prayers are forms that involve only meditation without any material or traditional elements. Pope Benedict invites us to open our hearts and to consider walking with our brothers and sisters who have lived before us, ready to meet Jesus as he speaks to us there.

For example, he says this about spending quiet time in Eucharistic adoration:

> In the Sacred Host, he is present, the true treasure, always waiting for us. Only by adoring this presence do we learn how to receive him properly—we learn the reality of communion, we learn the Eucharistic celebration from the inside. Here I would like to quote some fine words of St. Edith Stein, co-patroness of Europe, who wrote in one of her letters: "The Lord is present in the tabernacle in his divinity and his humanity. He is not there for himself, but for us: for it is his joy to be with us. He knows that we, being as we are, need to have him personally near. As a result, anyone with normal thoughts and feelings will naturally be drawn to spend time with him, whenever possible and as much as possible" (*Gesammelte Werke* VII, 136ff.). Let us love being with the Lord! There we can speak with him about everything. We can offer him our petitions, our concerns, our troubles, our joys. our gratitude, our disappointments, our needs, and our aspirations. There we can also constantly ask him: "Lord, send laborers into your harvest! Help me to be a good worker in your vineyard!"[89]

About the Rosary, he says:

> To be apostles of the Rosary . . . it is necessary to experience personally the beauty and depth of this prayer, which

is simple and accessible to everyone. It is first of all necessary to let the Blessed Virgin take one by the hand to contemplate the face of Christ: a joyful, luminous, sorrowful, and glorious face.[90]

And in the prayer of the Church, the Liturgy of the Hours:

The Liturgy of the Hours is another fundamental way of being with Christ: here we pray as people conscious of our need to speak with God, while lifting up all those others who have neither the time nor the ability to pray in this way. If our Eucharistic celebration and the Liturgy of the Hours are to remain meaningful, we need to devote ourselves constantly anew to the spiritual reading of Sacred Scripture; not only to be able to decipher and explain words from the distant past, but to discover the word of comfort that the Lord is now speaking to me, the Lord who challenges me by this word. Only in this way will we be capable of bringing the inspired Word to the men and women of our time as the contemporary and living Word of God.[91]

And, finally, we can open our hearts so that God can speak to us through all that surrounds us. Here the Holy Father speaks extemporaneously at the end of the Lenten retreat given to the Roman Curia, reflecting on what he heard and saw that prompted his own prayer:

During your first conference, I became aware that in the inlay of my *prie-dieu*, the Risen Christ is shown surrounded by flying angels. These angels, I thought, can fly because they are not regulated by the gravity of the earth's material things but by the gravity of the Risen One's love; and that we would be able to fly if we were to step outside material gravity and enter the new gravity of the love of the Risen One.

You have really helped us to come out of this gravitational force of everyday things, to enter into this other gravity of the Risen One and thus, to rise to on high. We thank you for this.[92]

To let Jesus be present to us in everything, ancient or new, in all that surrounds us, in all that we meet: that is prayer.

In the Name

The goal of Christian prayer is the goal of the Christian life— union with Jesus Christ. This union leads, of course, to joy and a sense of fulfillment. But as Pope Benedict has pointed out, if our own personal universe of emotion and need forms the walls of the room in which we pray, we will undoubtedly be misled and will end up not serving Christ but only ourselves.

For service, in the end, is the whole point. Meeting Jesus in prayer leads us to his heart, which is not a heart of sitting still and feeling okay about who we are. It is a heart of radical, sacrificial love.

On Ash Wednesday of 2008, Pope Benedict called on Christians to enter into that heart, not only for our own sake, but for the sake of the world:

Prayer is a crucible in which our expectations and aspirations are exposed to the light of God's Word, immersed in dialogue with the One who is the Truth, and from which they emerge free from hidden lies and compromises with various forms of selfishness. Without the dimension of prayer, the human "I" ends by withdrawing into himself, and the conscience, which should be an echo of God's voice, risks being reduced to a mirror of the self, so that the inner conversation becomes a monologue, giving rise to self-justifications by the thousands. Therefore, prayer is a guarantee of openness to others: whoever frees himself for God and his needs simultaneously opens himself to the other, to the brother or sister who knocks at the door of his heart and asks to be heard, asks for attention, forgiveness, at times correction, but always in fraternal charity.

True prayer is never self-centered; it is always centered on the other. As such, it opens the person praying to the "ecstasy" of charity, to the capacity to go out of oneself to draw close to the other in humble, neighborly service. True prayer is the driving force of the world, since it keeps it open to God. For this reason, without prayer there is no hope but only illusion. In fact, it is not God's presence that alienates man but his absence: without the true God, Father of the Lord Jesus Christ, illusory hopes become an invitation to escape from reality. Speaking with God, dwelling in his presence, letting oneself be illuminated and purified by his Word introduces us, instead, into the heart of reality, into the very motor of becoming cosmic; it introduces us, so to speak, to the beating heart of the universe.[93]

CHAPTER NINE

MEETING JESUS
IN EVERYDAY LIFE

*Of course, this is always a great adventure, but life can be
successful only if we have the courage to be adventurous,
trusting that the Lord will never leave me alone, that the Lord
will go with me and help me.*[94]

W hat has your day been like so far? Did you get the kids to
school? Is dinner planned? Are you overwhelmed at work?
Or anxious about getting—or losing—a job? How is your health?
Your spouse's health? Your children's? Tired? Missing anyone?
Wishing someone would go away? How many things did you
worry about today? Are you going to be able to sleep tonight?

Life is . . . life. God puts us here for a reason, we know, but
sometimes that reason becomes murky, or the demands and busyness of each day take on a life of their own. When that happens,
it is often difficult to rediscover the hand of God—even if we can
remember a time when that hand was very clear and present to us.

Those of us who aren't priests or religious or even lay church
employees might be tempted to look at those who are with envy
at times. After all, keeping Christ at the center of daily life is so
much easier for them—it's their job!

But those who work in the Church, either lay or religious,
find it just as challenging to keep Jesus at the center of their daily

doings as the rest of us. They are just as tempted to put him aside in favor of their own egos and priorities or to forget him in their dealings with others. Or, they may come to associate spiritual matters with the "job" mentality, from which they long to escape at the end of the workday.

A Christian's call to dwell in Christ doesn't just apply to Sundays or even our private prayer time—or the times that life is fitting our plan and we are in control. Jesus is with us always—which means that every moment of every day, no matter what our vocation, at any stage of life, he stands at the ready. What can we do to clear our hearts and heads so that we are ready to meet him as well? And what will it mean? Might there be a cost?

Follow Me

This separation of Christ from the grind of daily life doesn't happen accidentally. It is entirely possible that this chasm we feel might be our own fault. It is not just that we are victims of events creeping up on us. We make choices. We establish priorities. We decide on a path and keep walking.

It is a radical thing, this being in Christ. Even those of us who would, if pressed, describe ourselves as faithful Christians might have some distance to go in our realization of it. After all, what went into your decision to be where you are today? Why are you in the relationship you're in? Why are you working where you are? Why are you engaged in the activities that occupy your time?

If our answer centers on words and phrases like *success* or *want* or even *fulfilled* or *satisfaction*—which is probably most of us—we are missing something. For Jesus doesn't actually call us to any of those things. Jesus calls us to follow him.

We can certainly follow him in almost any path that's out there—that's the point of this chapter—but if the primary end goal of our decisions is our own satisfaction, happiness, and security, we might consider if we have really let Jesus all the way into our lives. Or do we have more in common than we'd like to admit with the rich young man, who went away sad? (Matthew 19:16-22).

Discipleship is handing it all over to God, and doing it all in his service and in service of those whom he loves. And before we are fathers, mothers, teachers, salespeople, doctors, artists, managers or students, each of us is a disciple of Christ.

On Palm Sunday 2007, the beginning of Holy Week, Pope Benedict addressed his words specifically to young people, but they apply to all of us. He invites us to tie our journey to that of the disciples, to follow Jesus all the way:

At the outset, with the first disciples, its meaning was very simple and immediate: it meant that to go with Jesus, these people decided to give up their profession, their affairs, their whole life. It meant undertaking a new profession: discipleship. The fundamental content of this profession was accompanying the Teacher and total entrustment to his guidance. The "following" was therefore something external, but at the same time very internal. The exterior aspect was walking behind Jesus on his journeys through Palestine; the interior aspect was the new existential orientation whose reference points were no longer in events, in work as a source of income, or in the personal will, but consisted in total abandonment to the will of Another. Being at his disposal, henceforth, became the *raison d'être* of life. In certain gospel scenes, we can recognize quite clearly that this means the renouncement of one's possessions and detachment from oneself.

But with this, it is also clear what "following" means for us and what its true essence is for us: it is an interior change of life. It requires me no longer to be withdrawn into myself, considering my own fulfillment the main reason for my life. It requires me to give myself freely to Another—for truth, for love, for God who, in Jesus Christ, goes before me and shows me the way. It is a question of the fundamental decision no longer to consider usefulness and gain, my career and success as the ultimate goals of my life, but instead to recognize truth and love as authentic criteria. It is a question of choosing between living only for myself or giving myself—for what is greater. And let us understand properly that truth and love are not abstract values; in Jesus Christ they have become a person. By following him, I enter into the service of truth and love. By losing myself I find myself. . . .

Dear young friends, how important precisely this is today: not merely to let oneself be taken here and there in life; not to be satisfied with what everyone else thinks and says and does. To probe God and to seek God. Not letting the question about God dissolve in our souls; desiring what is greater, desiring to know him—his face . . . [95]

This discipleship can happen in any way of life, in any stage of life. Priests and those in religious life witness to the totality of self-giving in a unique way. But the truth is that any of us—in any home, any classroom, any workplace, in a married relationship or single, young or old—not only can, but are called to let him be our guide and the voice to which we answer. As the pope says—and it's worth repeating—we cannot merely let ourselves "be taken here or there in life" or be "satisfied with what everyone else thinks and says and does."

This is radical, even if on the outside we may look like everyone else. The radical nature of it does not lie in complete withdrawal from the world, although for some it might. It involves letting our lives be completely guided by the loving hand of Jesus for the sake of the world. Be different, Pope Benedict frequently says. Be unafraid: "Today as in the past, it is not enough to be more or less like everyone else and to think like everyone else. Our lives have a deeper purpose."[96]

Life's Stages

Jesus meets us in our lives, inviting us to follow him in joy and find even deeper joy. We can meet him at any time in life and in anyone—there is no special age or stage of life in which Jesus is more fully present than any other. Pope Benedict speaks often of the face of Christ in children:

In the face of the tiny Jesus, we contemplate the face of God, who does not reveal himself in strength or power but in the defenselessness and frail condition of an infant. This "Divine Child," wrapped in swaddling clothes and laid in a manger with the maternal care of his mother, Mary, reveals all the goodness and infinite beauty of God. He shows the fidelity and tenderness of the boundless love with which God surrounds each one of us.

This is why we celebrate Christmas, reliving the same experience as the shepherds of Bethlehem. Together with so many fathers and mothers who toil constantly every day, facing continuous sacrifices, let us celebrate with the little ones, the sick and the poor, because with the birth of Jesus, the heavenly Father responded to the desire in our hearts for truth, forgiveness, and peace.

And he responded with such great love that we find it surprising: no one could ever have imagined it if Jesus had not revealed it to us!

The amazement that we feel in the face of the enchantment of Christmas is, to a certain extent, reflected in the wonder of every birth and invites us to recognize the Child Jesus in all children, who are the joy of the Church and the hope of the world.[97]

Moved by sentiment and the natural cuteness of little ones, this might strike us as not too great of a challenge. But remember that Jesus' declaration that one must be like a child in order to inherit the kingdom (see Mark 10:15) was an extremely strange thing to say in the ancient world. In the Roman world of the first century, children were nonpersons, and childhood was demeaned in general. The Christian reverence for life, based on the belief that we encounter Christ in others, including children, was a startling, even ridiculous claim.

Pope Benedict speaks frequently to young people and calls them to see the presence of Jesus in their own lives, and to respond to it. Adolescence and young adulthood are curious times. We are enthusiastic and idealistic in ways that we will never be again, yet we are also tempted to put off the real, serious business of turning our lives over to Jesus until we are older and have other adult responsibilities as well. Don't wait, Pope Benedict told young people in Brazil in 2007:

My appeal to you today, young people present at this gathering, is this: do not waste your youth. Do not seek to escape from it. Live it intensely. Consecrate it to the high ideals of faith and human solidarity.

You, young people, are not just the future of the Church and of humanity, as if we could somehow run away from the present. On the contrary: you are that young man now [see Matthew 19:16-22]; you are that young man in the Church and in humanity today. You are his young face. The Church needs you, as young people, to manifest to the world the face of Jesus Christ, visible in the Christian community. Without this young face, the Church would appear disfigured.[98]

Marriage and family, as stressed and as fractured as they can be, are among the most important places we encounter Jesus.

Pope Benedict uses the example of Priscilla and Aquila, friends and co-workers with St. Paul (see Acts 18), to make this point:

> This couple in particular demonstrates how important the action of Christian spouses is. When they are supported by the faith and by a strong spirituality, their courageous commitment for the Church and in the Church becomes natural. The daily sharing of their life prolongs and in some way is sublimated in the assuming of a common responsibility in favor of the Mystical Body of Christ, even if just a little part of it. Thus it was in the first generation, and thus it will often be.
>
> A further lesson we cannot neglect to draw from their example: every home can transform itself into a little church. Not only in the sense that in them must reign the typical Christian love made of altruism and of reciprocal care, but still more in the sense that the whole of family life, based on faith, is called to revolve around the singular lordship of Jesus Christ.
>
> Not by chance does Paul compare, in the Letter to the Ephesians, the matrimonial relationship to the spousal communion that happens between Christ and the Church (cf. 5:25-33). Even more, we can maintain that the apostle indirectly models the life of the entire Church on that of the family. And the Church, in reality, is the family of God.[99]

He also reflects on his own upbringing to show how all of us—children and parents and extended family—meet Jesus there:

Yes, I thank God because I have been able to experience what "family" means; I have been able to experience what "fatherhood" means, so that the words about God as Father were made understandable to me from within; on the basis of human experience, access was opened to me to the great and benevolent Father who is in heaven.

We have a responsibility to him, but at the same time he gives us trust so that the mercy and goodness with which he accepts even our weakness and sustains us may always shine out in his justice, and we can gradually learn to walk righteously.

I thank God for enabling me to have a profound experience of the meaning of motherly goodness, ever open to anyone who seeks shelter and in this very way able to give me freedom.

I thank God for my sister and my brother, who with their help have been close to me faithfully throughout my life. I thank God for the companions I have met on my way and for the advisers and friends he has given to me.

I am especially grateful to him because, from the very first day of my life, I have been able to enter and to develop in the great community of believers in which the barriers between life and death, between heaven and earth, are flung open. I give thanks for being able to learn so many things, drawing from the wisdom of this community, which not only embraces human experiences from far off times; the wisdom of this community is not only human wisdom; through it, the very wisdom of God—eternal wisdom—reaches us.[100]

In a culture and society so hostile to the gospel, we might be tempted to structure the ideal family life as a walled fortress, one closed in on itself. Pope Benedict's vision is far more expansive and not at all closed. All Christians are called to go out into the world, for this is what Jesus came to do, this is what his body does—live in the world, bringing Good News. Our life as families echoes the life of the Church in a very small but significant way: we live in the love of Jesus present among us so that we are strengthened to go out in mission.

Witnesses

When St. Paul describes the body of Christ, he points out that it has many members, with different functions, all important (1 Corinthians 12:18-31). We all meet Jesus in whatever way of life to which he calls us, and we meet Jesus in every circumstance, if we are open.

In that body, priests and religious have their specific part to play. As he addresses groups of seminarians, priests, bishops, cardinals, and religious, Pope Benedict frequently speaks of the role of self-sacrifice in this vocation. All of us are called to give ourselves over to Christ as his disciples, but religious witness to this in a particularly concrete way:

He calls people of all times to count exclusively on him, to leave everything else behind, so as to be totally available for him, and hence totally available for others: to create oases of selfless love in a world where so often only power and wealth seem to count for anything. Let us thank the Lord for giving us men and women in every century who have left all else behind for his sake, and have thus become radiant signs of his love. We need only think of people like Benedict and Scholastica, Francis and Clare of Assisi, Elizabeth of Hungary and Hedwig of Silesia, Ignatius of Loyola, Teresa of Ávila, and in our own day, Mother Teresa and Padre Pio. With their whole lives, these people have become a living interpretation of Jesus' teaching, which through their lives becomes close and intelligible to us. Let us ask the Lord to grant to people in our own day the courage to leave everything behind and so to be available to everyone.[101]

They are witnesses to the radical belonging that awaits us all:

Your way of living and working can vividly express full belonging to the one Lord; placing yourselves without reserve in the hands of Christ and of the Church is a strong and clear proclamation of God's presence in a language understandable to our contemporaries. This is the first service that the consecrated life offers to the Church and to the world. Consecrated persons are like watchmen among the People of God who perceive and proclaim the new life already present in our history.[102]

For this to bear fruit, for it to be real and effective, the priest and religious—from the humblest Poor Clare to the most celebrated cardinal—must be totally centered on Jesus Christ, not his or her own ambitions or strengths:

Dear friends, this is also the true nature of our priesthood. In fact, all that constitutes our priestly ministry cannot be the product of our personal abilities. This is true for the administration of the sacraments, but it is also true for the service of the Word: we are not sent to proclaim ourselves or our personal opinions, but the mystery of Christ and, in him, the measure of true humanism. We are not charged to utter many words, but to echo and bear the message of a single "Word," the Word of God made flesh for our salvation. Consequently, these words of Jesus also apply to us: "My doctrine is not my own; it comes from him who sent me" (John 7:16).

Dear priests of Rome, the Lord calls us friends, he makes us his friends, he entrusts himself to us, he entrusts to us his body in the Eucharist, he entrusts to us his Church. Therefore, we must be true friends to him, we must have the same perception as he has, we must want what he wants and not what he does not want. Jesus himself tells us: "You are my friends if you do what I command you" (John 15:14). Let this be our common resolution: all of us together, to do his holy will, in which lies our freedom and our joy.[103]

Go Forth

A little boy races around the house, destroying the order I had so carefully constructed. An unexpected meeting disrupts my plans at work. My children or my parents or my siblings or even my spouse break my heart. Traffic drives me crazy. Parishioners don't appreciate me. School is hopeless. What I am doing seems as far away from Christ as anything can be. I am small; no one notices me. It is all noise, but no substance; the world moves on and I have no idea what it means.

There are times when God seems absent from all of that busyness, from the pain and shattered goals, from the drudgery. And yes, there are times when God seems absent from the success, the good fortune, the achievements, and the satisfactory investment numbers.

But he's not. The Lord is present in all of it, just as he was present in the busy crowds in Palestine, in the workshops and marketplaces of Nazareth and Capernaum, among the tradesmen, the politicians, the beggars. As he was present among those deemed successful and those deemed failures, among the powerful and the rejected. As he was present when people shared meals, celebrated festivals, buried the dead, cleaned house, harvested crops, mended their nets, and gathered for worship. As he was present to families, to single people, amid running, laughing children. He is present in love, present with the gift of freedom and reconciliation, the gift of a love that transforms, frees, and empowers us to let go and give as he does.

Jesus is present in our everyday lives. But he does not force awareness of himself on us. His presence is not a magical one. If we want to become more deeply aware of Jesus, we have a part to play and choices to make:

Life is not only given at the moment of death and not only in the manner of martyrdom. We must give it day by day. Day after day, it is necessary to learn that I do not possess my life for myself. Day by day, I must learn to abandon myself; to keep myself available for whatever he, the Lord, needs of me at a given moment, even if other things seem more appealing and more important to me: it means giving life, not taking it.

It is in this very way that we experience freedom: freedom from ourselves, the vastness of being. In this very way, by being useful, in being a person whom the world needs, our life becomes important and beautiful. Only those who give up their own life find it.[104]

And when we do this, when we take this stance of openness, we discover something astonishing. Life is so much bigger, joyful, and, yes, fulfilling, than it was when we thought "self-fulfillment" was the best we could aim for:

What does "to be converted" actually mean? It means seeking God, moving with God, docilely following the teachings of his Son, Jesus Christ; to be converted is not a work for self-fulfillment because the human being is not the architect of his own eternal destiny. We did not make ourselves. Therefore, self-fulfillment is a contradiction and is also too little for us. We have a loftier destination.[105]

CHAPTER TEN

MEETING JESUS IN
SUFFERING AND DEATH

*In baptism, in the company of Christ, we have already made
that cosmic journey to the very abyss of death. At his side and,
indeed, drawn up in his love, we are freed from fear. He enfolds
us and carries us wherever we may go—he who is Life itself.*[106]

I vividly remember the first time death entered my consciousness as something more than an abstraction.

It was well before anyone I knew had actually died. I was
twelve years old, lying in my bed one night, when it hit me: there
would be a time in which I—as the "I" there in my room—was
no more. It would end for me. Seventy, eighty years from then,
life would go on, the world would turn, and I would not be
around to see it.

I was petrified, despondent. Normally introverted and reserved,
I couldn't hold in my emotions, which drew my mother's attention. She sat with me for a while, comforting me. I don't know
what she said, but it helped—at least for the time being.

Suffering and death—our own suffering, the suffering of
a child, the death of one, the deaths of many—these realities
surely have the power to call into question everything we have
been thinking about during the course of this book. Where is
Jesus then?

It is the fundamental question. Even St. Thérèse of Lisieux on her deathbed, even Mother Teresa of Calcutta faced it as they experienced the feeling of absence, the fear of the unknown, and the pain of physical and emotional suffering.

Where is Jesus?

I Thirst

There are no easy answers, of course. Job's questions about his own suffering were answered, not with a series of propositions or a position paper on God's part, but by God's presence and more questions, tossed back at Job. Where were you, God asks, when the world was created? Where were you? (See Job 38–42.)

But in Jesus, a different sort of answer to that question is offered. Propositions and position papers play no role in this answer either. Presence, too, is the answer: God's presence in the midst of human suffering, and another question, not from the wind and storms, but from a human voice: *My God, my God, why have you forsaken me?* (Matthew 27:46).

We meet Jesus in suffering because Jesus suffered, and because of our baptisms, he dwells within us. In him, we are embraced in love and brought to the other side, where suffering is no more:

God's love for us, which began with creation, became visible in the mystery of the cross, in that *kenosis* of God, in that self-emptying, that abasement of the Son of God which we heard proclaimed by the apostle Paul in the first reading, in the magnificent hymn to Christ in the Letter to the Philippians [2:6-11].

Yes, the cross reveals the fullness of God's love for us. It is a crucified love which does not stop at the scandal of Good Friday but culminates in the joy of the resurrection and the ascension into heaven and in the gift of the Holy Spirit, a Spirit of love through which, this evening too, sins will be forgiven and pardon and peace granted.[107]

No, we do not get an easy answer to the question of why in any of its forms: Why me? Why them? Why not me? Why now? But the answer we do receive leads us to the presence of Jesus in our suffering and the suffering of others:

> Through the cross of Christ, God made himself close to the peoples, he came out of Israel and became the God of the world. And now the cosmos kneels before Jesus Christ, and this is something we too can experience in a marvelous way today: on all the continents, even in the most humble of huts, the crucifix is present.
>
> The God who had "failed" now through his love truly brings man to bend his knee and thus overcomes the world with his love.[108]

In our own suffering, our eyes are drawn to Jesus on the cross. We see there, not only comfort, but the reality of love:

> But the Lord also knocks with his cross from the other side: he knocks at the door of the world, at the doors of our hearts, so many of which are so frequently closed to God. And he says to us something like this: if the proof

that God gives you of his existence in creation does not succeed in opening you to him, if the words of Scripture and the Church's message leave you indifferent, then look at me—the God who let himself suffer for you, who personally suffers with you—and open yourself to me, your Lord and your God.[109]

So how do we meet Jesus in our suffering? We turn to him in comfort, and we see his own suffering. The sight of Jesus' loving sacrifice calls us to walk with him and tells us, with great clarity, how much God loves us:

The Lord took his wounds with him to eternity. He is a wounded God; he let himself be injured through his love for us. His wounds are a sign for us that he understands and allows himself to be wounded out of love for us.

These wounds of his: how tangible they are to us in the history of our time! Indeed, time and again he allows himself to be wounded for our sake. What certainty of his mercy, what consolation do his wounds mean for us! And what security they give us regarding his identity: "My Lord and my God!" And what a duty they are for us, the duty to allow ourselves in turn to be wounded for him!

God's mercy accompanies us daily. To be able to perceive his mercy, it suffices to have a heart that is alert. We are excessively inclined to notice only the daily effort that has been imposed upon us as children of Adam.

If, however, we open our hearts, then as well as immersing ourselves in them we can be constantly aware of how good God is to us; how he thinks of us precisely in little things, thus helping us to achieve important ones.[110]

The world does all it can to keep suffering at bay and to hide its eyes from death, a stance that only serves to increase suffering and strengthen death's power to paralyze us, even as we still breathe.

There is one place, however, where illness and suffering do not hide, but come out into the open, walking slowly, pushed in chairs or even carried on cots, on a slow pilgrimage toward hope: Lourdes. In 2008 Pope Benedict visited Lourdes and spoke of the role of suffering in the life of one who belongs to Christ:

> Christ imparts his salvation by means of the sacraments, and especially in the case of those suffering from sickness or disability, by means of the grace of the Sacrament of the Sick. For each individual, suffering is always something alien. It can never be tamed. That is why it is hard to bear, and harder still—as certain great witnesses of Christ's holiness have done—to welcome it as a significant element in our vocation, or to accept, as Bernadette expressed it, to "suffer everything in silence in order to please Jesus." To be able to say that, it is necessary to have traveled a long way already in union with Jesus. Here and now, though, it is possible to entrust oneself to God's mercy, as manifested through the grace of the Sacrament of the Sick. Bernadette herself, in the course of a life that was often marked by sickness, received this sacrament four times. The grace of this sacrament consists in welcoming Christ the healer into

ourselves. However, Christ is not a healer in the manner of the world. In order to heal us, he does not remain outside the suffering that is experienced; he eases it by coming to dwell within the one stricken by illness, to bear it and live it with him. Christ's presence comes to break the isolation which pain induces. Man no longer bears his burden alone: as a suffering member of Christ, he is conformed to Christ in his self-offering to the Father, and he participates, in him, in the coming to birth of the new creation.[111]

Eternal Life

Death looms in all of our lives. Some of us have lived more intimately with it than others. Perhaps we have come close to death ourselves, or been in the presence of someone who has died, or engaged in that corporal work of mercy we call "burying the dead"—caring for what is left with respect for what God has made.

There is no question that to face death and commit to seeing the other side that Jesus promises is an act of faith. None of us reading these pages has ever traveled to that other side and returned. We cannot know what it was like in the same way that we can know what it is to visit Chicago, for example, or give birth, or even come close to the brink of death itself. It is in the company of this reality that we must finally and absolutely confront the issue that has lurked for so long: who is this Jesus of whom we speak, in whom we say we believe?

146

If he is only a teacher, even his most powerful teachings cannot really be trusted as I face death, for there are many teachers who have taught many things. Why believe him and not them?

If he is one in whom I believe because belief in him joins me to others on this earth and gives me a ticket to various rituals that bestow a particular identity, what good is that ticket when my skin is cold and my body is lowered in the ground?

If his story gives me comfort now, but is no more or less true than other stories that others share, what fruit can the story bear for me when my ears can no longer hear them?

Throughout this book, we have listened to Pope Benedict "propose" Jesus of Nazareth to us. He has not proposed a useful idea, an interesting story, or a profitable life plan. He has proposed a Person, the Son of God who really lived, died, and rose, and who lives *now* and who can be known *now* and who is Lord of creation *now*.

Faced with the void, I must ask: do I really believe that?

Because if I do—if Jesus is the Lord who is with me now, who forgives me, who guides me, who gives me his very life in Eucharist, whose every word in the gospels is directed at *me*, then there is no void. *Where, O death, is your victory? Where, O death, is your sting?* (1 Corinthians 15:55).

This is the joy of the Easter Vigil: we are free. In the resurrection of Jesus, love has been shown to be stronger than death, stronger than evil. Love made Christ descend, and love is also the power by which he ascends. The power by which he brings us with him. In union with his love, borne aloft on the wings of love, as persons of love, let us descend with him into the world's darkness, knowing that in this way we will also rise up with him. On this night, then, let us pray: Lord, show us that love is stronger than hatred, that love is stronger than death. Descend into the darkness and the abyss of our modern age, and take by the hand those who await you. Bring them to the light! In my own dark nights, be with me to bring me forth! Help me, help all of us, to descend with you into the darkness of all those people who are still waiting for you, who out of the depths cry unto you! Help us to bring them your light! Help us to say the "yes" of love, the love that makes us descend with you and, in so doing, also to rise with you. Amen![112]

ENDNOTES

All homilies, addresses, and audiences of Pope Benedict were taken from the Vatican Web site at www.vatican.va.

1. Homily, Inauguration Mass, April 24, 2005.

2. Homily, Inauguration Mass, April 24, 2005.

3. Joseph Ratzinger, *Milestones: Memoirs 1927-1977*, trans. Erasmo Leiva-Merikakis (San Francisco: Ignatius Press, 1998): 8. Reprinted with permission of Ignatius Press.

4. Alessandra Borghese. "The Heart of Joseph Ratzinger's Bavaria," *The Catholic Herald*, 16 May 2008, (http://www.catholicherald.co.uk/features/f0000259.shtml.

5. *Milestones*, 19-20.

6. *Milestones*, 36.

7. Gianni Valente, "Tradition and Freedom: The Lectures of the Young Joseph," *30 Days* (March 2006), (http://www.30giorni.it/us/articolo.asp?id=10284).

8. Letter to Bishops accompanying the release of *Summorum Pontificium*, July 7, 2007.

9. *Deus Caritas Est*, 1.

10. Christmas Greetings to the Roman Curia, December 21, 2007.

11. General Audience, March 22, 2006.

12. General Audience, May 17, 2006.

13. Address, University of Pavia, April 22, 2007.

14. Encounter with Youth, April 6, 2006.

15. Homily, Easter Vigil, March 22, 2008. l

16. *Spe Salvi*, 3.

17. Address, Vigil, World Youth Day, August 20, 2005.

18. Address, Welcoming Celebration, World Youth Day, July 17, 2008.

19. Meeting with the Clergy of Aosta, July 25, 2005.

20. Homily, Inauguration Mass, April 24, 2005.

21. Homily, World Youth Day, July 20, 2008.

22. Christmas Greetings to the Roman Curia, December 21, 2007.

23. Homily, Pastoral Visit to the Roman Parish of Santa Maria Consolatrice, December 18, 2005.

24. *Spe Salvi, 12.*

25. Homily, Pentecost Prayer Vigil, June 3, 2006.

26. Homily, September 10, 2006.

27. Address, Meeting with Representatives of Other Religions at the United Nations, April 17, 2008.

28. Homily, Pentecost Prayer Vigil, June 3, 2006.

29. Address, Congregation of the Doctrine of the Faith, February 10, 2006.

30. Address, Heiligenkreuz Abbey, September 9, 2007.

31. Meeting with Young People and Seminarians at St. Joseph's Seminary, Yonkers, New York, April 19, 2008.

32. Address, Synod of Bishops, October 6, 2008.

33. Meeting with Young People in Genoa, May 18, 2008.

34. Address to Bishops of Switzerland, November 7, 2006.

35. Meeting with the Clergy of Rome, February 22, 2007.

36. Address, Synod of Bishops, October 6, 2008.

37. Meeting with the Clergy of Rome, February 22, 2007.

38. Address, the Roman Major Seminary, February 17, 2007.

39. General Audience, November 14, 2007.

40. Address, Visit to the Major Roman Seminary, February 17, 2007.

41. Address, Visit to the Major Roman Seminary, February 17, 2007.

42. General Audience, November 7, 2007.

43. Address, Synod of Bishops, October 6, 2008.

44. Gianni Valente, "Tradition and Freedom: The Lectures of the Young Joseph," *30 Days* (March 2006), accessed at http://www.30giorni.it/us/articolo.asp?id=10284.

45. Meeting with the Clergy of Rome, February 7, 2008.

46. General Audience, March 29, 2006.

47. Homily, Parish of St. Anne, February 5, 2006.

48. Homily, Vespers, Cathedral of Munich, September 10, 2006.

49. General Audience, March 15, 2006.

50. General Audience, May 10, 2006.

51. General Audience, August 24, 2005.

52. Homily, Pentecost Prayer Vigil, June 3, 2006.

53. Vespers, Cathedral of Notre Dame, Paris, September 12, 2008.

54. General Audience, December 10, 2008.

55. Way of the Cross at the Colosseum, Good Friday 2005.

56. Homily, St. Patrick's Cathedral, New York City, April 19, 2008.

57. Homily, Palm Sunday, March 16, 2008.

58. Prayer Vigil with Young People, Loreto, Italy, September 1, 2007.

59. Address, Meeting with Young People of Sardinia, September 7, 2008.

60. Address to former students before Mass, August 31, 2008.

61. Homily, Easter Vigil, March 22, 2008.

62. Homily, Baptism of the Lord, January 11, 2009.

63. Homily, Easter Vigil, April 15, 2006.

64. Meeting with Children in St. Peter's Square, October 15, 2006.

65. Homily, Pastoral Visit to Our Lady Star of Evangelization Parish in Rome, December 10, 2006.

66. Homily, World Youth Day, Cologne, August 21, 2005.

67. Homily, Corpus Christ, June 15, 2006.

68. Homily, Corpus Christi, June 7, 2007.

69. Homily, Corpus Christi, May 22, 2008.

70. General Audience, August 2, 2006.

71. Homily, First Sunday of Advent, November 30, 2008.

72. Homily, Vespers, First Sunday of Advent, November 29, 2008.

73. Homily, Vespers, First Sunday of Advent, November 26, 2005.

74. Homily, Midnight Mass, December 24, 2006.

75. Homily, Fest of the Baptism of the Lord, January 11, 2009.

76. General Audience, Ash Wednesday, February 21, 2007.

77. General Audience, Ash Wednesday, February 6, 2008.

78. Homily, Palm Sunday, April 1, 2007.

79. Homily, Mass of the Lord's Supper, April 13, 2006.

80. Address, Way of the Cross at the Colosseum, March 21, 2008.

81. Homily, Easter Vigil, April 15, 2006.

82. General Audience, March 26, 2008.

83. Homily, May 7, 2005.

84. Homily, Piłsudzki Square, Warsaw, Poland, May 26, 2006.

85. Meeting with Roman Clergy, March 2, 2006.

86. Reflection, Synod of Bishops, October 3, 2005.

87. Homily, Mass with Bishops of Switzerland, November 7, 2006.

88. *Spe Salvi*, 33-34.

89. Vespers, Basilica of Saint Anne, Altötting , September 11, 2006.

90. Meditation, Pontifical Shrine of Pompeii, October 19, 2008.

91. Vespers, Basilica of Saint Anne, Altötting , September 11, 2006.

92. Address, Conclusion of Lenten Spiritual Exercises, March 3, 2007.

93. Homily, Ash Wednesday, February 6, 2008.

94. Meeting with Youth, April 6, 2006.

95. Homily, Palm Sunday, April 1, 2007.

96. Homily, Basilica of Mariazell, September 8, 2007.

97. Address to Children of Italian Catholic Action, December 21, 2006.

98. Address, Meeting with Youth in São Paulo, Brazil, May 10, 2007.

99. General Audience, February 7, 2007.

100. Homily, Mass of Thanksgiving in Remembrance of the Pope's 80th Birthday, April 15, 2007.

101. Homily, St. Stephen's Cathedral, Vienna, September 9, 2007.

102. Homily, World Day of Consecrated Life, February 2, 2006.

103. Address to the Clergy of Rome, May 13, 2005.

104. Homily, Mass for Ordination of Priests for the Diocese of Rome, May 7, 2006.

105. General Audience, February 21, 2007.

106. Homily, Easter Vigil, April 7, 2007.

107. Homily, Penitential Celebration with Youth, March 29, 2007.

108. Homily, Mass with Bishops of Switzerland, November 7, 2006.

109. Homily, Palm Sunday , April 1, 2007.

110. Homily, Mass of Thanksgiving in Remembrance of the Pope's 80th Birthday, April 15, 2007.

111. Homily, Basilica of Notre-Dame du Rosaire, Lourdes, September 15, 2008.

112. Homily, Easter Vigil, April 7, 2007.

This book was published by The Word Among Us. For nearly thirty years, The Word Among Us has been answering the call of the Second Vatican Council to help Catholic laypeople encounter Christ in the Scriptures—a call reiterated recently by Pope Benedict XVI and a Synod of Bishops.

The name of our company comes from the prologue to the Gospel of John and reflects the vision and purpose of all of our publications: to be an instrument of the Spirit, whose desire is to manifest Jesus' presence in and to the children of God. In this way, we hope to contribute to the church's ongoing mission of proclaiming the gospel to the world and growing ever more deeply in our love for the Lord.

Our monthly devotional magazine, *The Word Among Us*, features meditations on the daily and Sunday Mass readings, and currently reaches more than one million Catholics in North America each year and another 500,000 Catholics in 100 countries. Our press division has published nearly 180 books and Bible studies over the past ten years.

To learn more about who we are and what we publish, log on to our Web site at **www.wau.org**. There you will find a variety of Catholic resources that will help you grow in your faith.

Embrace His Word, Listen to God . . .

www.wau.org